The author was born in 1884. Florence Margaret Somerville Laing was the second youngest of her five siblings. Aunt Flo (our great great aunt) was the frailest of all her siblings. At an early age her parents were advised that she would be frail due to having had scarlet fever, diphtheria, and rheumatic fever. They were told that she should enjoy a quiet life. Flo wanted to be a nurse but too frail to train so she started looking after children instead.

Flo left England for India in 1920 having telegrammed her family to let them know what she was doing. She never married and spent last two years of her life living in Edinburgh with a younger sister. Flo died in 1984 just two months short of her 100th birthday.

We dedicate this book to Aunt Flo for writing this travel log and for entertaining us with tales every time we met her. We thank our dad Angus Douglas who was her great nephew for saving these books of memories and our mum who patiently typed and pulled it all together.

And to Anne and Fiona for enabling this to be published.

Florence Margaret
Somerville Laing

GREAT GREAT AUNT FLO'S TRAVELS

AUSTIN MACAULEY PUBLISHERS™
LONDON • CAMBRIDGE • NEW YORK • SHARJAH

Copyright © Florence Margaret Somerville Laing 2024

The right of Florence Margaret Somerville Laing to be identified as author of this work has been asserted by the author in accordance with sections 77 and 78 of the Copyright, Designs and Patents Act 1988.

All rights reserved. No part of this publication may be reproduced, stored in a retrieval system, or transmitted in any form or by any means, electronic, mechanical, photocopying, recording, or otherwise, without the prior permission of the publishers.

Any person who commits any unauthorised act in relation to this publication may be liable to criminal prosecution and civil claims for damages.

All of the events in this memoir are true to the best of author's memory. The views expressed in this memoir are solely those of the author.

A CIP catalogue record for this title is available from the British Library.

ISBN 9781035822058 (Paperback)
ISBN 9781035822065 (ePub e-book)

www.austinmacauley.com

First Published 2024
Austin Macauley Publishers Ltd®
1 Canada Square
Canary Wharf
London
E14 5AA

We would like to thank Austin Macauley Publishers.

Early in 1886, I accompanied my parents on a sea-voyage, round by the Cape of Good Hope, from Glasgow to Melbourne. The S.S. "Loch Garry" was one of the old windjammers which mostly carried cargoes of wool from Australia. She normally took three months but time is no object when you only require a restful holiday. Mother had two married sisters and two married brothers who had settled in Australia, so she looked forward to a re-union.

My first recollections were of our train stopping at such a funny little station – so unlike Broughty Ferry, Portobello, or those which were familiar to me at home. The railway lines seemed to have been laid on a cutting between endless scrub which wound round huge blue gum trees with lovely red and white blossom. Fern trees and wattle grew everywhere.

While father was arranging for our baggage, a tall man leading a horse came up and introduced himself as mother's brother-in-law. He thought that my mother would ride on Paddy's back! As she did not care for that idea, he rode and took me up on the saddle in front of him.

When my uncle and aunt were first married, they lived in Japan where my uncle had a post as navigation instructor to the Japanese Navy. My aunt was the only British woman and felt the loneliness so much that he was persuaded to resign from the British Navy and accept a grant of land in Australia.

By the time we arrived at "Budgeree", my aunt and her family (now five in number) had settled in their new home. From the original two-room hut was now built a long veranda, at the end of which had been added three or four bedrooms. Their cow, "Buttercup", roamed around outside the house and they had a few hens and ducks to provide eggs and I enjoyed helping my aunt to feed them and gather the eggs.

Grange, who helped my uncle with felling trees, tilling the ground and keeping the scrub down, lived in a small hut near us. He had gone with uncle some years before, cleared the scrub until they were able to make a clearing and mark off their claim. I remember going with my cousins to pay him a visit and he gave each of us a huge slice of plum cake that he had made himself and me remembering it all these years, shows that it must have been good!

After building a two-roomed hut, my uncle fetched my aunt and their baby son from Melbourne. This was "The Bush" and for those living in it, one might say that it was a real Robinson Crusoe life – very different to what my uncle and aunt had been accustomed to, but much like those of our early settlers.

To get to school, my two elder cousins had to cross a creed, by means of a log, laid across to act as a bridge. Like most boys, they loved teasing me. One way was when they killed a snake, they would hold it up on the end of a pitchfork. I preferred to play with my baby cousin on the veranda. I loved watching the many coloured birds and furry animals. For a child, mine was an ideal life and my father loved it there. I am afraid that my mother often longed for home and my brother and sisters who were parked between school and relations back in Scotland.

While up in this part of Australia, we visited Sale, where I was taken terribly ill with what I imagine was diptheria and the town of Bairnsdale where we went to the races. I was standing in a wagonette watching a race. "Robin" was evidently the favourite for, like a child, I became very excited and joined in with, "Come on, Dobbin, come on." Whether Dobbin, alias Robin, won or not, I cannot say.

By now we had been three years in Australia and when my parents decided to leave, my father was lucky in getting home on the "Loch Garry" for we liked the captain and felt that we knew the other officers – also, she was a comfortable boat. This time it was a cargo and we were the only passengers. Being the only child, I was much made of. This time we were to go round by Cape Horn, so for us it was like Chichester and Rose sailing round the world! Travelling with only cargo, we had no doctor and no stewardess. To mark that well in my mind before getting far on our way, I developed a bad attack of bronchitis. The captain insisted on sending for the doctor at the nearest port. Being before the days of a helicopter, an order was made to lower a boat. Shortly, Dr. Figg – for that was his name – arrived. With a name like that, one would imagine that his treatment would be very nice. It certainly cured me, but it was very drastic. I was placed in a very hot bath round which was draped, tent fashion, a large blanket. After drying, fly blisters were applied. However, the kindness that I received helped me to forget the pain and be happy.

I had had my fourth birthday before leaving Australia and had received a doll's house, but no furniture. The captain had a lot of little picture scraps which he gummed on the walls, mother made little curtains and the ship's carpenter, who must have been very neat fingered, made little chairs and a table, a bed, two small chairs and a cot for the baby. When I was well and able to run about, he made a safety swing which was hung up in the saloon. He also made a skipping rope which was useful on calm days when I could skip up and down on the lower deck. Going round Cape Horn, it was often rough and very cold. Captain Horne found a lovely pair of moccasins which fitted and kept my feet beautifully warm. There was always a mate off duty who would offer to take me by the hand and let me see the parrots and lovebirds that belonged to the sailors. There was also a monkey that amused me. One day, an albatross landed on the deck. Another day, we were surprised when a shoal of flying fish fell beside us and later, one of the sailors presented me with wings from one that he had caught and dried for me. We saw whales and seals at times, but nothing came up to the excitement of when we were followed by a shark. It was agreed that the sailors were to be allowed to catch it. A huge lump of ham was fastened to a huge hook which was lowered into the sea. I was very sad because bedtime arrived before it was caught. However, the captain bribed me to go by promising that when it was caught, he would keep it for me to see in the morning. He was true to his word and next morning, I wasted no time in putting my clothes on and going down to the deck. There lay a horrible looking fish with such a cruel mouth. I believe I felt rather relieved when it was heaved back into the sea. Well, as can be imagined, it was a very happy time for such a little girl and three months never felt too long or going too slowly.

At last we arrived at the docks in London. It seemed so different to the quiet of the Melbourne suburb of Brighton-on-Sea, where another uncle and aunt lived and Hawthorne, where the little girl I used to play with lived, who had a cherry tree in her garden. There were my other friends who had a lovely nursery with a rocking horse and endless toys. London seemed so busy and with no time for a little girl of nearly five years. I wished myself back in Australia where the sun shone and Bairnsdale where my little boy friend lived. No, my first impression of London was that everyone was in a hurry. I had just made my first purchase, a lovely sailor doll, when a man rushed past, bumped into me and off went poor jack tar's head. He was a British jack tar too! I felt very angry and the man never paused to say that he was sorry!

My grandfather's father was a tobacco merchant in Montrose. During his time, ships laden with tobacco came from the West Indies, and Montrose was a very busy little port but the blockade during the American War interrupted the ships getting through. Subsequently, the channel filled up with silt and the ships were unable to reach the shore. Montrose eventually became a holiday resort.

About 1820 raw jute was arriving at Dundee from India. This helped to take the place of the cotton shortage by being woven into rolls of coarse cloth, table cloths and towels. Afterwards, power looms took the place of hand looms, the latter being used for the fine work. When in his early twenties, my grandfather joined an uncle in Dundee. Later, when working on his own, he built a factory and installed the second power loom in the city. When my parents returned from Australia, we joined him at a small place about three miles out of Dundee, where he had been living for the last few years.

When we arrived home, I was very excited to find my brother, who during these past three years had been only the photograph of a little boy in a sailor suit, which I would kiss and say "goodnight" to before hopping into bed. Then there was my grandfather, another uncle and my grandfather's sister, Margaret. After Aunt Jane's death, the Montrose home was sold and Aunt Margaret came to make her home at Kelly. It was a large party of people for a little girl to arrive amidst, but I soon settled down and looking back, can truthfully say that I spent three very happy years at Kelly field. There was plenty of room for my brother and me to roam around. There were four fields, so between cattle and sheep and the odd field that had to be ploughed and harrowed and later, corn sown, when it was ready for cutting, we loved to be allowed to join in and help and very soon learnt how to bind and stack up the stookies and while they remained for a final drying, we loved playing hide and seek among it. My sisters were at home for their summer holiday so we had a big party. In my early days when there were no combine harvesters, there was much more that a child could help with; especially when it came to leading; when my brother or I would be allowed to guide a horse with its load and then when the stacks were ready, we would be allowed to pull on the cords until we reached the top. I remember when it was oats that were being threshed and sufficient would be sent to the millar to be turned into fresh meal for our porridge and oat cakes and bannocks. It was kept in a large kist in the kitchen.

There was also a large garden with plenty of fruits which we enjoyed to the full; an orchard, hedges and trees that were full of bird life. There was a putting green where we could also play croquet and a grass tennis court, so that, although we had few toys, we never lacked for something to do. On wet days, we passed the time playing in the summer houses but most of all we enjoyed hiding under the laurel tree which had a doorway cut in front. It touched the ground all round and formed a tent. Inside we had a garden table and two chairs and we could play tea parties or make a jeweller's shop, using chains of flowers – mostly daisies and dandelions – for jewellery. Our pets were two tortoiseshell cats and a goat. Our constant companion was Rover, my uncle's fox terrier, a long suffering creature. Sometimes we would make a harness for him and fasten the traces to a toy cart making him pull it along the country road, much to the amusement of the cottage children on their way to school. They would say, "Oh my, look at the dog." As I have said, we never wearied.

Our next move was when our sisters left school and joined us in our new home – a house about ten miles from where my grandfather lived. It was in a pretty part of Forfarshire and I was still able to cycle along and see grandfather and my old aunt. My one joy was that from my bedroom window, before hopping into bed, I could watch the light from the Bell Rock lighthouse that had been built by R. L. Stevenson's grandfather. I felt that it was guarding me as well as the many sailors off our rocky coast. I made friends with the family at the manse – a friendship that was to be a lifelong one. We shared our pleasures and always were welcomed in one another's homes.

Never having been very robust, measles and complications left me even less so. The doctor said that I was to be allowed to run wild for a year. My friends being at school, time hung heavily on my hands until Saturday came round. I seemed to pass a lot of my time in the field behind my home, herding a sow that belonged to our washer-woman. The school authorities seemed to be quite easy and no-one had heard of eleven-plus! However, by eleven, it was thought that I should go to school in Melrose where the doctor thought the climate would suit me better than Dundee. I did not like school and always looked forward to the holidays when I would be able to see my friends again.

The years passed. My brother was working and as I was nearly seventeen. I felt that I would like to be independent. Not being strong enough for nursing – which is what I would like to have done – and without a scholastic training of any sort, my mother did not think that I had any prospect of work. Fortunately, a cousin of mine, who had two small children, suggested that I should go to help her with them and so gain experience. I lived with her as one of the family member for two years and in that time I realized that I was fond of children and had chosen a career which was to prove a success. My cousin's husband was a minister in a lovely part of South Scotland. They lived in a beautiful old-fashioned manse and I found them to be very kind and friendly but after two years, I felt that I must make some money.

I went as a nursery-governess to a family not far from Edinburgh. There were five youngsters and what a jolly family they were. I taught the youngest lessons and supervised the elder ones after they had come home from school. While I was with this family, King Edward VII and Queen Alexandra came to Edinburgh. The streets along which they drove were lined with troops. My brother-in-law was one of those with the Forfar and Fife Yeomanry and of course, other Scottish Brigades and volunteers were there. The escort was a regiment of Lancers which was stationed at the old Piershill Cavalry barracks. (Redford barracks were not built until after the first war). A window on the route had been engaged and we had an uninterrupted view of the parade. I remember the King's smile as he doffed his plumed hat. Behind the troops there were such crowds of people and after they were in position, no one was allowed to move until the procession had passed on. We were lucky, as our two maids had arranged for a very comfortable lunch to be brought and we were able to enjoy this whilst waiting for the King to arrive. After the King and Queen had passed, the crowd was allowed to disperse and we were able to make our way back home.

A house had been rented for a month during the summer at Ramsey in the Isle of Man and with us came our cook and housemaid. Endless hedges of fuchsias bordered the road and there was a long, sandy beach where we spent many hours and where I had my first sight of Pierrots. Knowing nothing about pop singers, I lost my heart to one of them. I very much doubt if he bothered about me! Maggie, our cook, always came with us in the evening so I was well chaperoned! After that holiday was over, Nan, whom I taught, was to join her sisters at school, so shortly afterwards, I went to another situation where there was a boy of six. He was a charming little boy, very musical, and how he enjoyed dressing up and acting at Christmas parties and pantomimes. He showed promise of art, as he only had to see a bicycle or engine and he could draw it in detail. This family were comfortably off and they had a lovely house in the country where we spent some happy times. In the holidays we would be joined by two cousins and a halfbrother, which always added to the fun! For the summer, we would go to their house in Ballantrae where we enjoyed bathing and swimming. The time soon came for my charge to go to prep school and at this point, I had made up my mind to be a nursery nurse. I felt that I did not like teaching but was fond of children. Soon I heard of a little boy of three and his baby brother of eleven months living at Colwyn Bay. They were beautiful children but unfortunately very delicate, so the doctor ordered that they should go abroad.

My next two moves were not successful and only lasted for a few months. At the first family, I found I had to cope with three unruly boys – which I found impossible – and with the next family, I was expected to do work not normally carried out by a nursery nurse, and I found it too tiring, and so gave in my notice. I then had the chance of looking after a little boy with an Army family. When I arrived at Okehampton, I wondered if I would like it or if I should have tried to persevere with the family in Sussex. I remained for eleven years and the parents were like another father and mother to me. We were in Okehampton for six months.

All the big guns were brought for their annual manoeuvres. The guns with their limbers were drawn by four horses. They were such beautiful animals and so well looked after. I often watched them being groomed and after being rubbed down with wisps of clean straw, an officer would rub the horse over to make sure that there were no loose hairs to be seen on his white gloved hand. I loved walking on the moor and seeing the forest ponies that roamed about, out of the firing line. They had caught the interest of Mrs. Welsh and other famous artists who painted them.

Before returning to London, we stopped at Bude for a fortnight at a sandy cove called Crooklets. The next six months were spent at Hounslow. There, my walks often took me along by Kneller Hall where the military bands were trained. The following six months, we lived at Battersea Park. A cousin of mine, who was a Norland nurse, lived in the same street so we were able to go for walks together. Part of our time we would spend in the park or in Chelsea Gardens. My boy loved talking to an old pensioner who would teach him how to salute and put him through his paces. At other times, the boys liked to go along the embankment and watch the barges chugging along the Thames, or Tower Bridge opening to allow the shipping to pass through.

Our next move was to Colchester, where we stayed for six months. At that time, the Army wore their coloured uniforms, which were so appealing to children. In those days, instead of cigarette cards and toy motors, children collected soldiers and knew the names of all the British regiments. Next, we went to Woolwich and, except for holidays, were stationed there for six years – partly with the garrison and partly at the arsenal.

The year was 1911. Much was going on in England at this time and we went on with our daily routine, although we would hear of the activities of the suffragettes and the clamouring in Ireland for the Ulster Counties to be handed over. There were many Ulster men in Woolwich, so we were able to hear the opinions of both parties and, in the background, we heard the muffled sounds of war. An assassination in Europe, followed by the breaking of a treaty and the invasion of Belgium. There were stories of women and children being ill-treated. What was Britain going to do? The King held a review of the Navy after which the sailors had 24 hours leave. All afternoon, I was in the children's playground listening to the band which was playing, whilst on the other side of the grounds, a set of tennis was being played by some officers, when a dispatch rider arrived. The game was interrupted to allow one officer to read the telegram. Next moment, the band struck up with the "Marseillaise" and we knew that France had declared war.

Then came Britain's declaration of war and the troops and sailors were all recalled and the Army and Navy were mobilised. It was surprising the change that took place. The look of depression seemed to disappear and all was stir and bustle. The soldiers who had assembled on the ground with their guns and horses began to move and we knew that they were on their way across the Channel. As they left, their places would be filled by other battery and other horses. In time, our horses would be replaced by those from Australia or America.

On 4th August, 1914, war was declared and mobilisation was in full force. That day, that I was to join my sisters at Ballater but I was unable to travel till nine days later. Before then, no official would guarantee that I would ever reach my destination. The government commandeered all trains and the railway, when I finally started off. I realised that there was a strange assortment of people in the carriage next to mine. I noticed that they took a great interest in the river Tyne as we crossed the bridge and when we reached Waverley at 4 a.m., I noted four police officers had handcuffed and marched off two of the party.

When I reached Ballater, it was a lovely day and I found my sisters had gone out for a picnic and the landlady was busy making a batch of delicious oatcakes. She wanted to go out and buy me two chops, but I was so sleepy that I felt unable to wait so suggested that she give me two of her oatcakes, after which I curled up in a bed and knew no more until I felt two pairs of eyes looking at me. This was the "Return of the natives". I rather shocked my sisters as I would knit whilst walking along the roads. One scarcely saw a car and most of the horses had been commandeered. There was this advantage – pedestrians had the roads to themselves. We met at the golf course where all the wives were engaged knitting socks and balaclavas. One woman's balaclava might have fitted her baby son but certainly not a Gay Gordon!

After a month at Deeside, I returned to Woolwich and it was while we were staying at Blackheath one night, that a Zepplin sailed over my head. It was just like an elongated balloon. It passed right over but dropped a bomb over the parade ground and two others further on, in each case, aiming rather wide. It was now 1915 and as the boy's father was now on active service; there seemed no sense in remaining where things were becoming hot, so we took a house near Bournemouth. The boy was at a boarding school until his health broke down, when he came home and had a tutor – an old army coach – who thought boys required no recreation. However, Jack became very fond of him and I think he was glad to have the chance of a job, for cadets were just being rushed through courses and into the Army. When we left Woolwich, our faithful cook gave me a few lessons and then, armed with a couple of cookery books, I took her job and she left to take up the making of munitions. After the naval review, her sailor boy arrived and was having tea with her when the fatal telegram arrived to order him to re-join his ship. Poor Emily that was the last she saw of him. He was lost at the battle of Jutland. In time, another young man tried to win her heart. At first, she refused him, he had not volunteered but had been turned down as unfit. She realised that there must have been many men who had wanted to fight for their country but were unaccepted. I was glad later to hear that she had married him and they were making a happy marriage. He was a joiner by trade and doing well.

Food was very difficult to obtain during the First War. Two or three weeks would pass before one could get butter or margarine and, when we could get it, it was horrid and only fit for cooking. We got some terrible maize flour that gave everyone tummy trouble. Meat required steaming in a bowl for hours and I heard of a school where the matron told of having to divide a rabbit between eight boys. Even with the shortages and bad food, nobody seemed to grumble and yet it was said that in the early months of 1918, Britain was afraid of being starved out. Those who remembered, realised that Mr. MacMillan was saying the truth, when he said, "You've never had it so good," to the country.

Very little seemed to happen in our quiet little part of England – troops were busy training, representing our own colonies and U.S.A. Jack's father would turn up at intervals. We would have an omelette that night! I remember he said that my omelettes were as good as any he got in France. It was on these occasions that his wife would ask him to go out shopping with his uniform because she wanted butter and it was surprising how, with his Blarney way, there was always a quarter of butter to be found on a shelf.

At last in this way, the last of the war years came to an end. I remember Jack rushed in on 11th November to say that an armistice had been signed. You can imagine how everyone felt. We heard London went mad, everyone was dancing in the streets, giving vent to their feelings as they had never done before. One dreadful thing that happened was a terrible form of 'flu', more like the plague, the germs of which must have come from the battle fields. As people were dancing at the

Victory Ball, they would suddenly be seized. It was so sudden that those who were fit to drive up to London would be in hospital at the finish and others would have to drive on the return. Some never recovered. A doctor would visit each house in every street and, every day, a ward would be opened in hospital to deal with the dozens of new cases. This terrible epidemic following a longed for victory at the end of four years of terrible warfare, stunned everyone. With the termination of war, our temporary house by the sea was broken up. Jack went to a public school. I had the offer of a housekeeper's post in London and while the house was getting a face lift, I put up in a little hotel in Russell Square and during that, time was laid up with a touch of this virus. My job fizzled out and as soon as I felt better, I decided to go home. I joined my former employers until they were advised to go to Palestine. I took another housekeeper's job with two nice ladies – mother and daughter. Epidemics were raging in Edinburgh – scarlet fever and diptheria. I fell a victim to the first and then caught the second, so I was obliged to give up working, temporarily I hoped.

When I returned home, our old doctor said I must have four months off work, but I was so longing to be back working with children that, after only two months, I agreed to go to stay with friends in London and help with their family. They lived in a nice part of London and I should have been happy and content. Happy I was, but not content. Everywhere there was a restlessness and I became restless too. I think what I missed was the comfortable houses that I had been in the habit of living in. I missed the old fashioned servant more than anything – who looked upon a nannie as someone special. One felt that a new class of servant had risen, who resented doing anything for you because you were working as they were. One morning, on being told for the third week running that there was no time for the maid to tidy my nursery, I felt rather disgruntled. I thought of the kind cook who would stop me before starting off on my morning walk, with a tray holding mugs of steaming hot chocolate for my three charges and myself, as she would say, "It's very cold and this will warm you." How different now! It was a nice sunny morning and my eyes, running down advertisements in the daily paper which I was reading, stopped when I noticed something which would be a change and an escape and a chance to see a bit of the world. Perhaps it was in my blood, for my maternal grandfather – the seventh of eight sons of a minister – who had all trained for the law, was not contented to follow that as a career. Instead, he went out to Canada where he met his wife. She was the daughter of an ex-Army officer who had settled in Galt, Ontario, after the Peninsular War. Also, my grand-uncle James, at the age of 26, toured two different countries in Europe and would have continued to Palestine, but after the ascent of Mount Sinai, took fever and died at Cairo.

Whatever was guiding my future progress, is hard to say. It ended in my accompanying a lady and her infant to India towards the end of December 1920. Roger's mother was very kind and allowed me to share in the deck sports and take advantage of any sightseeing to be done so that I was able to enjoy the voyage as well as attend to my work.

The first few days of our voyage were uneventful. The Bay of Biscay was surprisingly calm. We went through the Straits at night and I remember thinking what a pretty sight the rock made, all lit up as with a million lighted candles. On entering the Gulf of Lyons, the sea was moving considerably and making ominous sounds, accompanied by those of dishes smashing. At breakfast, I noted that the tables were all laid with wooden partitions called fiddles. Into each fiddle was laid cutlery and plates and cups required for your meal. The chairs were all screwed to the floor so once you got to your chair, you felt on terra firma! Many passengers took to their bunks and were not seen until we reached port. Very few of the passengers were at lunch and even though it was Christmas Day, a gentleman and I were the only representatives for dinner that night! I noted that he seemed to enjoy his meal, but I was a little shy of plum pudding that night!

Early next morning we entered harbour. One heard the usual sounds of ropes and chains, the sailors shouting to one another and the slowing down of engines. We had reached Marseilles and were to remain there for two days so there would be plenty of time to see a bit of the town. However, until the doctor had passed the boat free of infection and all passports had been examined, no-one was allowed ashore. The overland mail had arrived on board and those who received letters were glad of them to pass the time while they were waiting to go ashore. Some of us threw pennies on to the quay for the children to pick up and we were amused by two young acrobats on stilts, a man with a concertina and marionettes, all hoping for something from the tourists coming off the boats. At Marseilles, I joined up with another girl and two young men, as they knew their way about, which was a great help. We took a tram car. Our cars back home had reached an old and dilapidated state, but this one seemed worse than I had seen before! We sat upstairs where it was very hot and full of smoke. I was sitting next to the window which had the strap used for opening the window. Unfortunately, the strap gave way and was left in my hand while the window lowered so quickly that the glass smashed! I felt very guilty, but my companion advised me to say nothing. If I did, such a fuss would be made that we would not be allowed to return to our ship. As one can imagine, that would have been a serious thing for each of us. Eventually, the tram took us up the steep hill to the long flight of steps that lead to Notre Dame. What a pull up we had and at the top was a nun holding a wooden box for alms. I carefully pulled out a florin and wondered why the mother looked so disgusted. My escort laughed and said, "No wonder!" Until he told me I had not realised that since the war, the exchange for a florin had dropped from 2 to 2 and a half d.

Before returning to our ship (was it the Herefordshire?) we stopped at a little tea shop and had some cakes which were up to all our expectations – as we were not sure what to expect after the scarcities at home. On leaving Marseilles, we noticed that we had picked a few more passengers who had travelled overland in order to avoid the Bay of Biscay. After refuelling, we sailed out of the Gulf of Lyons under quite different conditions as we had when we entered. There was a beautiful blue sky overhead and a calm blue sea which lasted until we reached Port Said. We arrived there very early on New Year's Day but not too early for Simon Artz. News must have gone round that our ship was arriving for immediately the whole shop was illuminated and as we entered the large oriental shop which drew alongside our boat, each assistant was standing behind the counter ready to serve the burra sahib and the burra logue. That was fifty years ago.

I was not travelling to India to buy presents, but I did buy a few postcards and posted my mail for home. I also bought some Turkish Delight, for which Simon Artz was always celebrated. some of it full of cashew nuts and delicious green nuts whose names I can't remember. Then my table companion and I wandered round. The bougainvillea was flowering and it was a sight never to be forgotten. That night, I think everyone was able to enjoy the New Year dinner. Being Scottish, I received a glass of delicious burgundy and of course had to join in a toast while my thoughts went to those at home. That night we went slowly down the canal. This narrow waterway, hardly wide enough to allow two large ships to pass one another, had a large stretch of sandy desert on either side. Once, three Arabs on beautiful horses rode up and had a look at us. Further on, we passed the remains of an army camp. A few chairs showing signs of the worse of wear, were all that was to be seen. There were a few soldiers still waiting to be de-mobbed who were so pleased to see us. The young men lined our deck and called, "A good new year to you," and with a laugh they answered back. After Suez and passing through the Red Sea, we reached Aden where we stopped for a few hours.

It had been decided that it was too hot to go on and we had had enough. A few passengers from the ship hired four or five taxis and drove along the coast to have a look at the oil wells. On their return, we were soon underway and sailed straight through the Indian Ocean to Colombo, reaching there before nightfall. We were very tired for there had been some delay in berthing and we had just been lying off the coast tossing about on a choppy sea. I was thankful to get into bed but it was Burns' birthday, and I remember that night well.

There were some gay Scots in a room below me celebrating the poet's birthday for all they were worth. Every time they landed up with 'Auld Lang Syne', I said to myself, "That's the end," – not a bit of it. "Let's take a cup of kindness yet," rang out yet again and so it continued until I fell asleep with the old familiar refrain ringing in my ears. Fortunately I awoke feeling fresh and with the baby, I went down to second breakfast. We were staying in a beautiful hotel. The dining room had a wide veranda onto which we could go through numerous French windows. Flowering trees and shrubs gave everywhere a cool look and large electric fans worked from the ceiling. Numerous small tables with snow-white tablecloths were laid ready for the guests. The waiters were Cingalese and wore white dhoties and I remember their hair was coiled up on the back of their heads and fastened with a beautiful tortoiseshell comb. A brother of a great English friend in Woolwich looked me up and we enjoyed meeting and having a drink – mine was my usual Nimbou Panni. We then went for an excellent meal. We started with fruits and what a selection there was to choose from – juicy oranges, pineapple, melon, mangoes, guavas, passion fruit and papayas. Soon it was time to go and after saying goodbye to my friend, I collected Roger and we went upstairs for a siesta and a bath and did our packing. Soon we were on our train that would take us across Ceylon to the north where we were ferried over to the most southern point of India. Roger's father brought his bearer with him to Colombo so he looked after us. He was most helpful and as we were so thirsty with the heat, got us a block of ice which he put into an ice-box where we kept soda water and drinking water. The baby and I shared one carriage. The two beds were quickly made up by our bearer whilst we were having dinner at a railway station. Each carriage had a shower and wash basin and toilet. I was able to hang a line across, so while we were travelling, baby's vest or nappy soon dried and as it was very hot, he wore no more clothing. As the fan was in action, a thin chuddha across his tummy was all that was necessary. One morning at 4 a.m., Roger's mother came from the adjoining carriage to say that we were passing Madura and if I would like to come out and see the temples. Being keen to see all I could, I quickly roused myself. As it was dark, we were just conscious that the train was taking us through great forests – probably teak. Here and there we would pass through villages and small towns with the most interesting architecture and occasionally we would stop at a railway station. I went to sleep again only to be awakened by a blacks face at the window and a voice asking if I wanted bananas! Wanting the baby to continue sleeping, I shook my head.

At last we reached Madras. The noise from a babel of tongues never ceased and one saw squalor all around. I was thankful when we all got into our car and left the sights and sounds behind. Soon we had left the tongas and bullock carts in the distance and we were driving along roads, under the shade of large purple trees near the beautiful Pacific, with catamarans, white surf and silvery sands. Along we went, passing through villages until we reached Somerford on the river Adyar. The last part of the road we drove under tall coconut trees – the trees the little boys used to climb like "Black Sambo" until they reached the coconuts. The servants had had word of our arrival and the old mali had strewn the drive with rose petals from the little white and pink ramblers – they, and wisteria grew everywhere, as if wild. All the ground was so sandy and dry that the mali had to depend on two or three hot beds and a few large flower pots in which he would have some multi-coloured cannas, which made a great show, until two cows made a bee line for them and 'crunch, crunch' was heard. In Madras, our servants wore long white shirts or ghotis and white cotton coats. On one occasion while we were at lunch, the butler heard this sound of crunching and I did laugh, for then he and the other servant simply pulled up their skirts above their knees and ran after the cows. It made me think of the Bible where it says, "And he girded up his loins and ran." Forty years ago was very much as it must have been in those far-off Biblical days. Water was brought up from the well in chattis. These went round in a wheel that was worked by a pair of bullocks walking round the well and, as they walked, they pulled a log that levered the wheel. Corn was threshed and ground in similar fashion. Clothes were washed by beating them on a stone. There was no piped water in the houses and a water man had a wooden pole on one shoulder, balancing two earthenware chattis. One's bathroom had a bit cut off by a concrete ridge to keep the water in. No water was wasted, for when one had finished washing, the water was tipped out where it ran into a water butt for mali and his plants. One important thing was a bit of wire netting over the hole so that no snake could enter in search of a drink. The water carrier had to heat the water, which he did in a very blackened chatti which was continually boiling on a wood fire. There was no coal but plenty of wood. Cooking was also very out-dated. The oven was in the earth and it was fascinating to watch the women their cooking.

Our house must have been very old and was on two storeys like most bungalows in Madras of that period. It had a wide veranda supported on white pillars surrounding the rooms that opened on to it. Up a wide staircase lead to a covered veranda with a parapet. On one side, one could look on to the drive. From the other verandas, one looked across the river Adyar. The bedroom, with a large electric fan that we slept under, and the morning room, were on this side but facing the top of the stair was a room with three large rooms off it.

I shall never forget my first experience of Madras. If I left my breakfast unprotected, a crow – and there were many of them – would come in and wolf it for me. In the daytime, I noticed that all round the cornice were little tails hanging down from the ceiling. I discovered that these were bats and at night, whilst I was having dinner, they would fly round and round. I would put my hands up and hope that they would not settle on my hair. In the bathroom and on the wall, I would see dear little lizards. It was a good thing that I didn't dislike creatures.

The lizards would slip out from behind the mirror. Coming up the stairs one day, I was startled by a snake slithering down the banister and then I was nearly knocked into by a mongoose chasing after it. It was only a grass snake and non-poisonous. One day, whilst I was sitting on the veranda, a small, but very poisonous snake, slipped out from behind some flower pots and I was just in time to tell Roger to stand where he was and call out to the butler, who very quickly killed it. The old mali always said that there was a cobra at the banyam tree and we knew a family of mongoose frequented that path, so we were very careful never to remain there when dusk fell as it was then that life in the jungle began to move.

After a morning cup of tea, when all was beautifully cool, we would go for a morning walk. Sometimes a friend from a bungalow not far from us and her charge would join us. We would go through our lovely compound with stunted shrubs over which trailed little climbing roses and wisteria. Here and there were hedges of prickly pear and clumps of casarima trees and we would continue until we came to a little sandy beach. After lunch, we all would lay down to a siesta, have a wash and after dressing and a cup of tea, were ready to go by car to the marina where we would join the other children who played on the sand until the mist would come down and the nurses would think it time to return to their homes. Sometimes there would be a party and what fun the children would have. Towards the end of April, the weather was warming up and the wives and families would move to the hills as it was unbearable for the Europeans to spend the summer on the low country.

It was my first experience of going up and living 6000 ft. up one of the ghats in South India. We went by train to the bottom of the ascent and, as our journey progressed and we went higher and higher, we felt the drop in temperature. Every so often, we would add an extra jumper to the children and oneself, until at the top, we were clothed as if for a walk over the Pentlands or English Dlowns. The road rose in hairpin bends, carrying us through wonderful foliage, strong growing fern trees and eucalyptus. In fact it is they that give the name to these hills – Nilgiri, meaning "Blue Hills". Little waterfalls were trickling down over the rocks as they would in Scotland, watering the little red tulips and maidenhair fern. After rising two or three thousand feel, one got such a wonderful and unforgettable view of the plains that stretched as far as one's eyes could see and the lights on the colouring were what you would find on a Turner landscape – those delicate mauves, mixed with pale pinks and pale blues.

We arrived at what was a most comfortable hotel kept by a Euro-Asian widower. It was called Glenview (the name of a school where I had received most of my education) and consisted of a collection of little bungalows, each being served from a communal kitchen and, as each guest had their own bearer with them, it was just like, "Home, Sweet Home." Our bearer got into disgrace for picking a bunch of lovely pink tea roses and decorating the sitting room with them. When I told the old proprietor that the boy had given them to me because he knew I loved roses, he was so delighted at my admiring them and said that I must send the bearer for more whenever I wanted them! Their name was "Morning Glory" and I was able to enjoy a garden full of home grown roses, even though the three Scottish ladies to whom it belonged had lived in Conor nearly all their lives. It gave me great pleasure after such a long time, to see such roses and smell their fragrance after having been so long away from home. While I was there, I heard that a cousin had lost his wife under very tragic circumstances. His children were at Kotagiri with a mutual connection whilst they were receiving treatment at the Pasteur Institute. I later spent a lovely ten days with these newly found relations in their home in Secundrabad Daggan. We also saw each other during the following hot weather when we both were in neighbouring bungalows in Kotagiri. Kotagiri was 10,000 ft. high – 4000 ft. higher than ConCor.

As the months passed, the weather became cooler and it was time to return to the plains. This time, as we went down the ghat, we had a very good driver who took the corners so well that the little boy did not feel sick. We thought so much of him that we made sure of re-engaging him for the following drive to Kotagiri! Going down, we reversed our routine and instead of adding to the wardrobe, we had to skin the rabbit until, when we reached the plains, we only had thin vest and cotton dress. It was good to get down and see those that I had not seen for the last six months. I found the Church folk were always friendly and there were the usual rounds of children's parties. Lady Willington, the Governor's wife, always went out of her way to meet anyone from home and was always there to lead off the first couple at the dances. Sometimes, I gave Murray's nurse a lift. She was fond of dancing and I enjoyed watching. The twosome had just come in at home and someone was able to let her see how it was done and it wasn't long before she was up and trying it herself! We left about midnight and found Mr. Strathy waiting to take us home. I had an introduction to Major Lorimer and his wife. Major Lorimer was at the General Hospital and they were always kind to those from home and gave me open house. Once or twice, Mrs. Lorimer invited me over for a weekend. What I enjoyed most was having ghota-hazri in bed in the morning. Only a curtain cut me off from the public gaze.

By now the hot weather had begun and really we should have left the plains but there was a delay in the arrival of a new push-chair. It ended in Roger's mother drawing a diagram of what we wanted and having it made at a local firm. It was very nice and comfortable for the baby and was much admired by other families in the hills.

That year we went to Corsley – a long forest bungalow – and shared it with two other families. Mary and Dan had a family friend looking after them while their parents were down in the plains. It was nice for me because, except for my child, I would have had no companionship. The bungalows were very much scattered. My friend Rhona was up in a bungalow about a mile from us with her children. Miss McPherson was very kind and kept an ear tuned to Roger so that I was able to go along and have supper with her. Bappoo, my bearer, was to come for me at 10 p.m. Ten came round but no Bappoo had arrived. Rhona's servants had shut up and left for the night. They had their own quarters where they slept and fed when off duty.

Rhona said if my servant did not turn up, I would have to spend the night with her for I could not go home by myself. At that moment, I heard voices. There was Bappoo and another man carrying two hurricane lanterns. Bappoo said he had seen a bear and was frightened, so went back to find someone to come with him. As we walked along, we heard a noise, like the branch of a tree breaking and the servants cried, "Siegrem, siegrem," which meant, "Quick, quick." I reminded them that they must keep with me. Next day, as we passed the tree, we found a large branch had been broken and I supposed Mr. Bruin had wanted to reach the pears! Our cook often roasted these jungle pears and with a thick syrup, we thought them very good.

One day, Dan had a birthday. We always had breakfast in a room with white washed walls, round which hung the heads of wild deer and animals that had been shot by a former. As it was "Little Master's" (the title he is known by in southern India) birthday, the heads of these animals were all garlanded with flowers and the chair that he was to use was also beautifully decorated. Mary too had her birthday while we were there but she decided that she would like hers to be held under a lovely deodar tree. Except for an entrance, the branches surrounded and touched the ground, making it resemble a tent. Two servants in their white coats and cummerbunds waited on us. A large white cloth was spread with china etc. just as it would have been if we had been in the house. The cook had made cakes that possibly had been chosen by Mary. There would be various jellies and plates of fudge etc. After tea, Mary's mother helped with sticks collected by the younger ones to kindle a bonfire, making sure that everyone was standing a safe distance from the flames, then each took hands as they went round to the chant of old favourites.

On another day, the children had, as a ploy, a rickshaw run to a tea-garden a few miles away, where the children were to be weighed on the huge scales which were used for weighing the baskets full of tea leaves. We hired three rickshaws, each with four coolies, two in front and two at the back. What a rate we went, up and down the little hills on which were rows and rows of tea plants and women all busy picking as one sees in pictures. On the way back, we stopped at the bakery and saw some dough ready to go into the oven. Each child was allowed to put a finger into a loaf and was promised that that loaf would be delivered next morning and they would see their finger imprinted.

Round Corsley were little hillocks on which hill guavas grew. When they were ready, we went and gathered them and our cook made delicious jam. Being a large party, we soon got through it. However, we always enjoyed gathering more and asking the cook to make more jam. He was always good natured and never grumbled. In fact, I think that he felt flattered to think we thought so well of the jam and were asking for more.

Although living on the edge of a deodar forest and miles from any township, we were a very happy party. We were even able to have a laugh one afternoon, while the children were resting, to watch our bull walk along our back doors under a washing line, where someone's pair of corsets were hanging. We saw him pull them down as he walked away and I noticed that they had disappeared down his throat – too far down to make an attempt at rescuing them, even if we had felt inclined.

While at Kotagiri, I had the chance of going to Ootagamund to spend the day with a friend. Ootagamund was where all the big box-wallahs from Calcutta and Madras spent the hot weather with their families. The governors and their retinues, the railway officials and their families all went to Ootagamund Hill Station during the hot weather. It was a large flat plateau, so races and point-to-point were held there and those who could afford it, had their horses, grooms and stable boys, brought up from the plains. The land was still under the British Raj. A time like that I like to look back on – a time of peace, a time when sahib was respected and memsahib and the baba-logue worshipped. When I went to Ootagamund, I went by the little mountain railway. The view from its landscape windows was superb.

At the end of my stay, Roger's mother was taken very ill with malaria and had to go down to the plains to be treated. She was not able to return and, soon after, it was cool enough for us to join her. By that time, Roger had a little baby sister and a good ayah was engaged to help so that I could still continue with Roger as before.

The Congress party was beginning to make trouble in South India. Ghandi was coming into the public eye but very little attention was given to him. If we asked if there was likely to be trouble in the city, the butler would shrug his shoulders and say, "No-one will want to hurt little master." We went on as usual and if there was any demonstration, it was not near where we lived. Lord Willingdon was Governor of Madras and Lady Willingdon was very interested in the Indian women who were welcomed at the Indian Lady's Club which she opened.

Another change that was taking place was the union of the Presbyterian and English Churches in South India. When I was in Madras, it was at the discussion stage but it eventually ended in a United Church for South India.

Owing to a change of plans, Roger's parents had to go home a year earlier than was originally planned. This time, we went by train from Madras, crossing central India to Bombay from where we sailed for home. We had ayah with us and she was a great help looking after the baby, while Roger and I were able to have a meal at a canteen. The waiter managed to bring a huge plate of curry for ayah as she only had time to fill her water bottle! Poor ayah, she was very sad at parting with her "Biba".

The railway lead through tropical trees and little villages. Through endless trees were great splashed of red which I was told was "Flame of the Forest" – a sight which I have never forgotten. I think it was on this voyage that we travelled on the "Nevasa". During the First World War, it was torpedoed but survived. Until lately, it was used by the National Trust for their cruises round the Scottish coast. Roger went ashore with his mother at Port Said, Marseilles and Gibraltar. I remained on board where I found it very entertaining. At Port Said there was the usual "Gippy" with the poor little chicken which everyone felt sorry for, the man who was diving for pennies and at Marseilles there was the usual puppet show, the couple on stilts and the concertina man. We arrived in Gibrattar. during the daytime and I was able to buy three lovely oranges – quite the finest that I have tasted. They must have just been picked from a tree for one had a fresh green leaf. It was night when we arrived at the uncle's home in Tamworth so both children were just slipped into bed where they continued sleeping. They woke up when my nursemaid came in with tea for me and a drink for Roger who could not make out who the stranger was. "Who is that lady?" he asked. When he was told "Alice" he asked, "Is she our new ayah?" It must have been very strange for him. The coal box was another attraction for he had never seen a fire on coal before.

Now we were in the Black Country, in the midst of the coal pits and potteries. It was March 1923 and this part of England was dismal and grey. Every morning Roger would say, "Will the sun shine today?" It was too much for me. After the lovely sun of India, I found it too depressing and very shortly had arranged another appointment with a family going out to Quetta. A friend I knew had been there and used to talk about it and had aroused my enthusiasm so much that I decided to see for myself.

It was an anchor boat that we sailed in and we found it very comfortable. I remember they had such delicious bread. It was like being on a private yacht. Besides our party, there was only a couple and a single girl who was going out to her uncle who was stationed in Quetta, so Mrs. Lakin took her under her wing. Being so few of us on board, we sat at the captain's table. Another privilege was that the weather being so hot, we were allowed to sleep on the deck where we just lay and looked at the stars. It was then that the captain pointed out the Southern Cross. The steward brought up our bedding at night but we had to be early astir because at about 6 a.m. the Lascars would be there with buckets and brooms waiting to scrub the deck. It meant dressing-gowns and run whilst the steward carried our bedding back to where it came from. I had nearly forgotten to mention that before we reached Port Said, we touched at Malta. Unfortunately, I had a bout of fever which only lasted for two days, but it meant that I had to stay in bed and was unable to join the party going ashore. There must have been a strike, or trouble of some kind, for the captain said that no ladies were to go ashore unless they had a man as an escort. The doctor was able to go ashore, so with two other men to make up the party, it was considered safe. That was the only time that a boat that I was a passenger on stopped at Malta, so it was my bad luck that I was unable to visit the shore as I had hoped.

Our visit to Port Said was just a case of exercising one's legs. The rest of the voyage was uneventful so we were able to relax and enjoy the warm weather on board. Finally we arrived at Bombay where John's father, with his bearer and Gurkha orderly were waiting for us. We spent that day at a hotel and left by the night mail for Lahore and from there we caught a train for Quetta. At Bombay we were dressed in tropical clothes and I remember Colonel Lakin saying that I would find it very cold. When I got out on the platform at Quetta, I was in a tweed costume and indeed it was cold. As soon as I reached our bungalow, I very quickly got into warm clothing and had to keep it on for the next two months!

Our bungalow was one of those on the Hana Road, a steep road that lead up the pass where it reached a river, which trickled down like a little burn at the side of the road. The malis's way of watering their gardens was most ingenious. Each gardener took it in turn and the mali whose turn it was, made a cutting in the turf which held the water back, so it slowly trickled through to the beds of spinach, broccoli, cabbages or peas, tomatoes or the flower beds. At night, the piece of turf would be replaced and at the next garden another piece would be cut and so on until the bottom garden had been reached, when the first mali would take over and so on until the hullah would dry up.

John and I enjoyed walking up this road. I felt amused at the way the orderly would appear and follow us at a respectful distance. He was the first Gurkha that I had ever seen and in appearance was frightening with his swarthy skin and Mongol look but after my years at Abbottabad, I learnt to admire them and realise how much their officers loved them. They are the most brave and loyal people as we were to find out in later years.

One day, I went down to the bazaar, having been advised by Col. Lakin to keep to the part patronised by the Europeans as there was one part considered unsafe for British people to wander about in. I found the bazaar most absorbing and spent many happy visits, walking around.

Unfortunately, John was very spoilt by his mother, which made him very unmanageable and his mother and I agreed to part as soon as I could find another job as they wished to engage an ayah. I think the ayah was to be an attraction because as a Colonel's wife, she had a lot of entertaining and an ayah would be useful as she would be able to be her maid as well.

I had no difficulty in obtaining another job. John's godfather knew that the wife of a brother officer required a nurse for his baby daughter, so that was how I came to look after Jean. She was such a lovely baby and full of character. Our bungalow was nearest the club and our morning walk lead us along a road which had a row of apricot trees on either side. It was beautiful when the blossom was out. The bungalow was swept away in the bad earthquake of '35. Like all the bungalows in that part of India, it had windows in the bedrooms near the roof. It gave protection from attacks by any of the tribesmen. It also had a door entering a hall with fly doors leading on to the veranda. At night, the jackals would howl. When this happened, Ben, a large bloodhound would push the fly door open and as he did, poor Peggy, a small whippet, would follow and get caught which would make her give a little yelp. When the hot weather came, I used to sleep with my door open onto the compound. Dear Peggy took it upon herself to guard us, possibly favouring Jean, because she would look upon the baby as something belonging to Sahib. She lay stretched across the doorway, so I felt that she would dare anyone to come near us. In the same way, she would lie under the pram if I were away and Jean was sleeping in the compound while I was in the nursery.

The days became very hot and I was glad to spend the afternoon on the veranda and in the evening enjoyed a drive in the desert. One came across holes from time to time when one felt the car and passengers being tossed like a pancake in the air. Unknown to me, the service at the Scottish Church was moved to an hour earlier start. Consequently one day, not aware of the alteration in time, when I arrived, I found the service almost at an end. Normally, I had to walk to the front of the church and sit in a field officer's family pew. At a glance, I saw no women folk Jocks all the way (a Battalion of the Argyles and a Battalion of the Black Watch). I was just going to retreat when a kindly Jock moved up and beckoned to me to take his seat.

Before long, the rain came and the nullah from the Hanna Pass flooded each compound as it rushed on its way, the water surrounding our bungalow and the mali and servants had to make cuttings to help it on its way. The horses that were out exercising returned and water was well up on their tummies. In that autumn, our regiment was moved up on the frontier to a very lonely place called Risalpur. The Scots Grays represented the British Army and the central India Horse.

We had a little English Church and at night about twelve of us would worship under three or six hurricane lamps hanging from the ceiling. The nearest approach to a shop was a general store and I could just reach it and walk back during my morning walk. There was also an aerodrome. The village was so small that it only consisted of one long street and, occasionally, living so close together, relations got a bit strained. Once, two Irish nurses were not on speaking terms and their charges were friends, so it was rather awkward. I was looked upon as the peacemaker because I pointed out that it was impossible for them not to meet, so common sense prevailed. The Irish fires went out and all was well.

On one occasion, when I had to go to my bank, I took a tonga, for it was four miles away. It was just like the pictures that one sees of the Khyber Pass – great rocks, behind which you expected to see a Pathan lowering a rifle at you. Our colonel who lived opposite us, had a very nice nurse for his little girl and I was quite glad of her company. On the way to Nowshera, we had to cross a river on a bridge of boats. The horse was not too sure of it and went at the rate of a hunt. It was about this time that the Regiment was on manoeuvres and of course the unruly Pathans thought they saw their chance. A few half-sick soldiers were looking after the wives and children. Each bungalow had an armed guard at night and there was a warrant officer during the day. After I had had dinner at the opposite bungalow and returned to our bungalow, I was so startled on my return by being challenged by the sentry, that it was fortunate that the bearer was with me, for I would never had been allowed to pass as I did not know the password. I got such a start when the sentry lowered his musket and gave me the challenge.

It was only six months since we travelled from Quetta to Risalpur. Part of the journey was past a very exposed part of country, through uncertain people. Jean's father had special permission to travel with us and we had our doors and windows carefully locked and he had a loaded revolver beside him. However, all was well, except that the horse box and shoes and two dogs got cut out somewhere on the journey. We arrived to find that the electricity had not been turned on and there was no furniture of any kind. I found a large china basin and a case of whisky which made a strong and steady seat, so I was able to bath Jean. However, the Adjutant's wife insisted on putting us up that first night. The lost horse box had arrived safely by the following day, but now that we were surrounded by the Frontier tribes who were reputed thieves, it was thought wiser to leave the horses at the lines. We were glad to have Ben and Peggy in the house. It gave us a comfortable feeling of protection. Everyone had been very busy and by the second night, electricity had been connected and what furniture we required obtained were from the store. The khansama said that he could give Miss Sahib dinner but it was to be difficult to arrange for anyone else. As is the usual custom after dinner ends, the servants came to salaam and you know then that they have left for the night. Jean was sleeping and I was sitting with a book or doing some sewing, when suddenly there was a terrible banging on my back door. Thinking that it was one of the wild Pathans, I rushed to the veranda hoping to see the orderly but almost as frightening as seeing a Pathan, an apparition in white, rose up and waved his arms and talked some gibberish that I did not understand. Thinking of the Mutiny horrors, I rushed back to Jean, rolled her up in a blanket and started up the drive, meaning to go along the road to the next bungalow. I had only reached the gate when Jean's father entered and was running towards me saying, "It is quite all right but I think you had better wait and see if we have another." I could not think what he was talking about but felt quite relieved when he explained that it was a slight earthquake. At the same time, the Chokidar, for that was who he was, held out a letter, which on reading, said that this happened every year but did no damage.

We stayed in Risalpur until April, when Ann was on the way. It was thought best to be home for the event. We had to say goodbye to Ben and Peggy but Nana, a lovely English sheepdog, was overjoyed to receive her late mistress back. We travelled on an Anchor liner, taking the boat train from Marseilles to Calais, stopping overnight in Paris. Cooks were arranging everything for us and the next morning, a man arrived at our hotel and wanted to take all our baggage so that he could get it through customs quickly and it was with great difficulty that I was allowed to carry Jean's bottle of milk and the minimum of necessities in a handbag. I don't think I have ever seen motoring equal to that of the taxi drivers. We rushed down narrow streets, round corners, hooting at any poor pedestrians in the way who skedaddled like some poor hens. Suddenly we drew up at a large building. Here I was asked to give Jean's precious bottle. The cook opened the bag and waved it at the official, explaining that this was nourishment for the baby. Bang went the taxi door and again the perilous rush until we reached the railway station. The French porters were very much taken up with Jean and certainly she was very engaging.

France still showed signs of war havoc. It was sad to see groups of blackened stumps where there should have been fruit trees full of blossom. Whilst going on board the cross steamer from Calais, we gathered that this was the first time in seven days that the boat had been able to do the crossing. We very soon realised that the storm was still on and portholes and hatches were all closed. I remember counting the waves as they crashed over us – three was bad but every seventh was terrifying as it swept over and around us. Everyone was sick and the poor stewardess could hardly keep on her feet as she went from one to another. Jean, lying on my knee, suffered too and cried and cried. When we reached Dover, we were relieved to see the white cliffs and more than grateful to the kindness of a policeman. It was as if he saw at a glance how things were when he heard the baby crying. He said to leave the baby with me and he would take her mother through the customs. He was back in no time, asked a few questions, took us along to where we got our train and spoke a few words to the guard who locked us into a first class carriage. After half an hour, we reached the house where Jean's grandmother lived.

Kent is a county that I have always loved and at this time, the cherry blossom was out and everywhere was just beautiful. The house was full of interesting history too. At one time it was a retreat house for the monks at Tunbridge Wells. There was a pond where you picture the Fathers fishing for Friday's dinner. Round the front of the house was a walled rose garden and you entered through an old studded oak door into a parquet hall, off which was a large parquet room with latticed windows and a huge open fireplace with a seat on either side of the peat fire beside which were brass dogs with tongs and poker and bellows lying near at hand. Over the mantelpiece was a coat of arms and the name of an original owner. I remained with Jean until Ann was born and taken over by a nurse whom I had known in Madras.

I then had a well-earned holiday and fixed up with a lady going to Amballa and Kasauli. These were both places that I knew something about and thought that I would like to see. I joined the family at Camberley where the maternal grandparents lived. It was a very comfortable house in the midst of the lovely country but before long we left England on the "Rajputana" on her maiden voyage. After leaving Tilbury, we ran into rough weather and battened down in a ship smelling of new paint. It was not a nice experience. Most people were sick and our stewardess was nearly run off her feet. Joan was very sick and her mother helplessly so. I was feeling very bad but I managed to keep going by sucking a finger of bread dipped in Worcester sauce. By evening, in spite of trying some cure, Joan's mother was in no better shape so, after some persuasion, she agreed to follow my idea of Worcester sauce (a popular one with those who have to work at sea) and it worked wonders, so much so that other passengers tried this cheap, non-healthy service cure. To show the severity of the storm, our pilot had to remain on board until he got into quieter waters off Plymouth. As we left the dock, our ship carried a small bit of the quay with her! The rest of the voyage was uneventful and before long, we arrived at Bombay. It was too hot to be walking about and we were all thankful to be on the train for the north and away from the crowds of cripples and beggars that collect at railway stations and dock sides. I always found the Indian trains so comfortable. The old bearer was there and looked after me and the children. At night, while we were having dinner, they would make up beds, fetch hot water from the engine and drinking water from a restaurant at the station where we had stopped and had dinner. When we left Bombay, our ice-box was supplied with ice and bottles of soda water. In addition, we had a big block of ice in a basin. Some of the trains had water running down the windows as one sees in fish shops. It all helped to keep things beautifully cool for, in addition, we had electric fans.

At last we reached Pindi, where we remained for three weeks. We had to remain in the cantonment because of an outbreak of smallpox in the bazaar. In fact, the first thing that we had to do next morning was to line up at the hospital and be vaccinated. I had been vaccinated so many times, that I think one would say that I was immune.

Our next move was to Kasauli. I remember the car was closely packed and a servant lay on the footboard on either side as we rounded hairpin bends and climbed the khud. It all felt rather dangerous. The tall deodars which lined the hillside took away from the steepness of the cliff and insecurity of it all. At last we reached Kasauli and were able to look about. It was a small hill station that the wives of the Royal Fusiliers and their families went to for the hot weather and men who had been ill were sent up to it to regain their health. A short distance, as the crow flies, over a duster of small hills, lay a large girls' school for the children of railway employees. Continuing on this hill road, one reached Simla, the hot weather quarters for the Viceroy and the Governor of Bengal.

I was charmed with all I saw in Kasauli. When we went for our walks, we would wander along between grassy land and beautifully coloured dahlias which were growing wild. Round the house, cosmos grew. One day, the children were going to a party and we stopped to let the syce pick some of the dahlias and decorate Joan's pony. It made a perfect picture, for with her lovely velvety brown eyes, she herself made the picture for she was very pretty. The small brown monkeys were very mischievous and often made the children laugh. They would leap up a tree, snatch a towel off the clothes line and tear off to another tree. Their eyes would light on a row of tomato plants and in a twinkling, they would snatch a lovely red tomato from the first plant, take a bite and throw the rest on the ground while they ran on to do the same to the next plant and so on until every plant had been attacked and nothing was left. One night, when the children were settled for sleep, I stood at the back door to enjoy a breath of air before darkness came down, when a string of monkeys ran across the grass. The first one hastened their footsteps when they saw me but the last one paused with such an impudent expression, put a paw to his head and salaamed, then ran forward to catch up with the rest of the troop.

Hanley Cross was the name of our bungalow and with its lovely view over the Simla hills, one felt drawn to it and yet there was an unexplained mystery about it. When we first arrived, we expressed surprise at the numerous bolts. Inside and outside were four inch bolts for drawing at the top and bottom of every door. At first I was busy with my work. A children's nurse in India had more responsibility and much of her work was different than at home. I had to sometimes cook the child's food and superintend the washing as well as supervise the ayah or nursery bearer. In spite of this, when at Kasauli, I had very bad luck. Andrew had trouble cutting his teeth; Joan, who went to a nursery school, developed whooping cough. Parents that we knew were congratulating me on Andrew escaping infection, it being the 21st day after Joan developed it. Next morning, Andrew became ill and I also fell ill to the infection. I used to be known as the nurse with whooping cough. Poor little Andrew was very ill and when he had a paroxysm, he would allow no-one but me to stay in the room with him. I felt extremely relieved when the two of us were better and on our feet again.

Another alarm I had was when their father was away on duty and their mother had joined a party who were going around doing theatricals for the Army families who had travelled north for the hot weather. This time, I observed signs of dysentery and when I sent for the doctor, he feared it was so and next day sent word that he would come up later and asked for me to have a syringe, boiled and ready for him. An officer's wife in the next bungalow was so kind and relieved me of Joan in the daytime and that night wanted me to lie down and let her sit up with Andrew, but he awoke to realize that she was there and began to cry so I was unable to leave him. Her husband had offered to send a cable to the mother, but it was very late when he arrived at the Dak office, it had closed. The station master was sympathetic and said he would put the message through. About one in the morning, I heard footsteps on the veranda and this was the mother of the baby. She was at the theatre when the cable reached her, waiting for her turn to go on stage. A friend who was in the audience offered to motor her home and she left the hall at once. It was a long and lonely drive, but I was very relieved to have her home to share the responsibility and help to nurse the baby who was very ill. It was weeks before one of us was able to leave his bedside. It meant constant nursing day and night. This, after the long spell of whooping cough, coupled with Andrew's time with teething and Joan, though she was very pretty, was a difficult child. She took a great deal out of one and required a lot of patience; I fear not easily given from one who was feeling worn out. I felt obliged to give in and apply for another post which I heard of.

Paddy, a little girl of two years – a dear little girl who reminded me of and behaved like a fairy. Unfortunately, her mother was quite the opposite! She had been told by the doctor that I was the best nurse in Kasauli and she took a violent fancy to me, and I and others who knew her, thought that all was to be well. She, taking me and the child, were to go to Kashmir. Kashmir was a part that I had read so much about and longed to see. However that pleasure was to be postponed for eight years. Small trouble broke out with China and, situated over the border from Kashmir, Major G. thought it wiser for his wife and child to go to England and be near her people. It was then I noticed how she would go through abnormal changes of temper for no apparent reason. One day, I would be told to go and then she would come and apologise and beg me to remain. The agreement was that I was to have my passage paid but that I was to remain for six months after my arrival in England. Six months seemed a short time, but it was the longest voyage and most miserable one from India that I ever spent. It is strange how something will turn up to help you at a time like this. Some would say it was luck but I would say it was providence.

A Colonel's wife who knew me when I was with her husband's regiment in Risalpur, ran into me one day on board ship when I was ironing and she said that if I could help her when I got to England. She would be only too pleased because she realised how impossible it was for me to continue. She gave me her address and told me to contact her if necessary. Before leaving India, I had the sad news that my mother had died and naturally, this added to my misery.

We arrived at Plymouth and from there we took a taxi across Devonshire to Clifton where we stayed at a boarding house where my employer's step-sister – an older woman, a widow and one I took to – lived. After that we heard of nice rooms at Croyde Bay Inn. At the time, Croyde Bay, which borders between Dorsetshire and Devonshire, was a charming little village, full of artists, who found its picturesqueness appealed to them. I must have stayed peacefully for some weeks for I remember spending the day at Barnstable. However there came another flare-up and when this time I was told I could leave, I hastened to take her at her word before conscience had time to change her mind. I packed my things, ordered a taxi to drive me the 30 miles to the station where I would catch my train for Edinburgh. I remember we stopped at Bath where we were told that we would have to go to Crewe and travel on another route as this line was blocked by the falling in of a tunnel at Birmingham. Two gentlemen in the carriage who were reporters, said to another girl in the carriage that they must be in Glasgow next day to represent their papers because Queen Mary was launching the "Queen Mary". They said if I cared to come with them, they knew how, by crossing Birmingham, they could reach another station and from there, continue their journey. When we reached Crewe, THEIR tickets were passed but the ticket collector said that I was travelling on the wrong line! He said that he would take no notice but that I might be turned out when I reached Carlisle. This was just what happened. In the early hours of the morning we reached Carlisle and sure enough I had to get out and while we waved goodbye, I tried to smile. Carlisle is a grey and dismal station at the best of times but with waiting rooms locked and the sun scarcely more than rising, it was not a cheery spot to be stranded in. At 6 a.m. the restaurant doors were swung back and a tea trolley was pushed through. *Cheers! A cup of hot tea,* I thought. Not a bit of it. "This is for first class passengers only." Do first class passengers feel the cold and thirst more than 3rd class that they have to wait until 8 a.m.? I am afraid that the boy was neither Irish nor Scottish and my sarcasm was quite lost on him!

It was a long journey and I was glad at last to get home. It was a sad home-coming for I had lost my mother and her death made a great blank in our family. After a short holiday, I went to London as I found this was the only way to get a satisfactory post. It wasn't long until I got what proved to be a very nice post. It was for a boy of two, with lovely Irish blue eyes and it was to be another posting to India.

In the hot weather, the family stayed in Karachi and in the cold weather, we joined the husband in Sukkur, reckoned to be, along with Tawk, the two hottest places in India. We were there while the copper dam was being built. It was known as Lloyds Dam, as after completion, it was hoped that there would be sufficient water to irrigate the whole Sind desert. The soil was so salty that in the morning it looked completely white and no vegetation was able to grow on it. Sukkur had a bad climate for Europeans. At first, John, the elder child, was ill and we thought that we would have to go home. However, with great care, he managed to overcome all the tummy troubles so common in the east. Being near the sea, the sticky heat seemed to be made bearable. In Sukkur, the judge had an old nanny for his little girl. She was an English woman and felt the loneliness very much and was so glad for my companionship. While up there, we managed to see one another once a week. Funny to say, she came into my life once or twice. The last time I heard of her was on our final return from India in 1943. I ran into a mutual employer on our troopship. He told me that his family was in Africa for the duration of the war and that nanny Maylott had retired and was living with a sister in Maidstone.

Going back to our life in Karachi, India became very unsettled. Bad riots were taking place and as we were sailing for England, we had a very nasty experience. On the way to the wharf, we ran into a mob and were obliged to turn and take another road. Next day, we heard that the military were obliged to fire on them, so we were very glad to have got away in time.

We went to a farmhouse for the summer. It was in beautiful country near Hazelmire, called Liphook. While I was away, my father had died, so I took a holiday with my sisters. At the end of my last term in India, I was not feeling very fit in health. It had been many years coming backwards and forth and began to think I should have a spell in the Old country. I got a very nice post looking after two children – twins, Richard and Ann. They were just like turtle doves. If Richard cried, Ann would refuse to suck her bottle! It was lovely watching them and how they throve. I felt very proud of them and it was with a sore heart that at six months, I felt obliged to resign.

In a weak moment, I had promised to return to my former employer should she want me to return in the future. If I had known what I had let myself in for, I would not have been so rash. One hears about interfering grandmothers, well, there was one here and she just made my life miserable. However, by looking after two boys and their baby sister, I enabled their mother to go to Sukkur and witness the opening of the Dam which was the first of its kind at that time and a great credit to our engineers.

The home of the twins was a small property in that beautiful part of England – the Cotswolds. The house was very comfortable and had a small but old-fashioned staff of servants, who looked after their master and mistress and the family. (In this case there were two families, for Richard and Ann had two half-sisters and a half-brother. Two of them I was afterwards to meet when in Sialkot in 1935. In the eyes of these servants, a nurse held a responsible position and in those days was treated with great respect and consideration. It was even noticed how polite the Colonel's springer was, should I come in close contact! Quite a contrast to how he would growl when the butler entered his room in the morning. It is the little things that one remembers. I can't remember the housemaid's name but she would always keep me supplied with fresh flowers and, knowing how fond I was of dandelion tea, gave me a private supply and told me to keep it for my early cup. On the night of the Hunt Ball, Miss Pauline came in to let me see the new dress that she was wearing for it. We were giving a dinner that night and several young couples were there before going on to the Ball. As they were going through the hall to the dining room, the same housemaid beckoned to me and, from a vantage spot, I got a good view. Mr. Peter and the other men in their pink jackets and the young ladies in their long dresses made a beautiful picture. As I moved away, the housemaid said how sorry they were to think that I was going away. They had thought that I would remain until Richard was as old as Mr. Peter and be able to see him going to the Hunt Ball. Mr. Peter was in Sialkot with the xix Lancers playing polo against the xviii Hussars. When Mr. Peter heard where I was, he called and had coffee with me. Next morning, his sister came round and told me about the twins. It was so nice to see them and get news of the twins. One so often wonders how their babies have grown up.

The war came that has left many blanks. Roger, I imagine, became a press photographer. When in the Indian St. John's Ambulance I met Lady Denning who had known me in Risalpur. She gave me news of Jean and Andrew. The former was studying for the stage and Andrew was at Eton. In a recent "Who's Who" I read that he had died of wounds. It made my heart ache and I think of him sitting in his pram watching the band playing and keeping time with his finger.

The last I heard of John and Robin and his sisters, was by meeting their father on a troopship returning from Durban. When war broke out, their mother took them to South Africa I wondered where they were. Michael's father writes articles for the Edinburgh Tatter so he has survived the war and Michael was not old enough to serve.

For a short while, I went to a family who were living at Rustington in Sussex. Two girls and a boy made up the family. Their father had been lost in an avalanche on Sonamarg in Kashmir. They were a charming family but I was restless. India was calling me. There were other parts that I wanted to see and I was feeling strong and ready to work again.

This time I obtained a post caring for two Caesarean babies. Peter was not expected to live and his mother could not afford a nurse for long, so she asked me to take him while she was waiting for Michael who was due in two months' time as she thought it would give Peter a better chance of surviving. He did surprisingly well and I had a photo of him when aged three.

He looked a fine boy. His father belonged to "The Tigers" and was stationed in India. Michael's father was in Hodson's Horse and when I took charge of Michael, the regiment was stationed at Sialkot. It was raised at the time of the Indian Mutiny and had much pre-Mutiny history. The Mutineers marched along the main road and, passing the Scottish Church Mission, murdered the missionary and his wife and their only child. I got to know the missionaries who were there in 1935. They very kindly asked me to spend two or three weekends with them and they told me where the missionary had lived. I believe the Church was standing at the time of the Mutiny.

Many of the bungalows in the cantonment were pre-mutiny. Some of them had very large compounds. Our bungalow was not pre-mutiny but the compound was part of what had been one. One night, I remember being conscious of voices on the veranda close to where I was sleeping. The voices were those of British children talking, to who might be their ayah. The British had long ago left India. I wonder if those phantom voices are still to be heard on that veranda. Is that faithful ayah still there with her beloved "Baba logue?" I like to think so.

The voyage going out to India was very much in the same order as on previous journeys; two days at Marseilles, which I always enjoyed. As we left the harbour, Michael's mother and I stood watching while another concertina player had his instrument ready beside him, and after enjoying the old man with his instrument and his daughters going through various steps and antics, we realised that the siren had gone and the ship was preparing for departure. Those on my ship struck up "The Marseilles" after which we left to our own National Anthem being played by the old man on the shore.

Our next stop was Port Said. It was a relief to go ashore and stretch our legs, although to me, Simon Artz was becoming very hackneyed. The bougainvillea was growing everywhere and it was lovely. As always, I enjoyed sailing slowly down through the Suez Canal. The sunsets were beautiful and always remain fresh in my mind. In the daytime, we saw three Arabs in their flowing robes, mounted on superb horses, galloping along the sand. Until we reached Port Said, the weather was cool. The sailors were all wearing their blue uniforms but when they reached Port Said, they changed into white drill. The passengers were glad of the awnings that protected them from the hot sun and would choose the coolest spots to place their deck chairs. We stopped for a few hours at Aden. No wonder it was always spoken of as the "Barren Rocks of Aden". There were a few taxis which were hired by some of the passengers who wanted to drive along the hot, sandy road to the oil wells. Most of the passengers and those with children remained on deck trying to make use of every whiff of air. Most of the children experienced prickly heat, which made them very cross and irritable and gave those in charge a few bad nights. No-one was sorry to leave Aden and continue their voyage to Bombay – a town that I have always remembered and have never tired of. It was an imposing town and one worthy of a great empire. There were comfortable hotels and residential areas, churches and colleges and European shops which were excellent. Two famous railways met here and one could travel for 5 to 7 days, and with a good bearer and a few tips to the railway staff, be most comfortable. I have been able to get jugs of hot water from the engine for washing and sometimes I would hang up a short line and while the train ran along, vests would soon dry. Other times the bearer would get a block of ice which in an old biscuit tin, if rolled in a piece of sacking, would help to keep the temperature down. Ice and bottles of soda water in the ice box was also a must. While the train was stationary, we would have time for a meal at the restaurant and while we were out, the bearer would make up our beds. When we returned, we found everything tidy and shortly afterwards the train would start off again. We stayed two nights at the Metropole Hotel, leaving very early to catch the frontier mail train. Part of the journey was familiar, but before long we had arrived at our new quarters. The cantonment was interesting. There was a British Cavalry regiment and a British Infantry regiment.

Each regiment had a mess for the bachelors and the married officers lived in old bungalows round a large maidan (common). The troops each had their own common. Hodsons Horse was close to our bungalow and I often sat where Michael could watch the horses training and exercising.

Our bungalow was typical of the rest. In front, a row of steps lead up to a lounge and off here lead one bedroom; behind the lounge was a dining room and servants' pantry etc. At each side was a suite of bedrooms and each suite had its own bathroom, if not two, and its own veranda. I had one bathroom but used the other as my nursery pantry. As each bedroom had a dressing room, I had mine for my bedroom and what was supposed to be a bedroom, I had turned into a nursery. It had a useful but quaint fireplace. I say quaint, for one day it fell to pieces and crowds of white ants rushed out from the plastered surround. When this happens, apparently you have to find the queen ant. We sent for a Royal Engineer who had an instrument and by listening through this, he was able to find where she was living. When his men went and destroyed her and her home, masons were able to come and build up our fireplace so that we could once more enjoy a fire. I must explain that at the time that we were in Sialkot, it was winter time and English flowers were blooming. There were rows of lovely sweet peas. It was a very enjoyable weather, just what one might have on any warm day at home but in the hot weather, the temperature might rise to 122 degrees in the shade and then the families and sick were sent to the hills.

During this weather, Michael had his birthday and what a lovely birthday party he had. There were two camels in the Regiment – they were used for dispatches – but on this afternoon, we were allowed to have one. I have a photo of

Mike sitting like a fly, in front of the rider. These particular camels, whenever they felt your foot in the stirrup, started to move and then with a long stride and unsteady gait, covered the ground. Being warned that those animals gave you no time to mount, I did not feel able for the required spring. Many British families, including nurses and children, would annually tour on camel and loved it, but they were accustomed to going at a more leisurely speed than that of a dispatch rider.

At this time, Michael was running a temperature. In India, a high temperature in a child may mean a warning of something developing and, again, may pass off in a matter of twenty-four hours. The doctor in charge of the Army families liked the child in the hospital where he would be near at hand for him in case of an emergency and the nurses' observation. I was allowed to stay with Mike and he had a little room with two beds for ourselves. In our case, we were very comfortable and Michael was soon himself again.

There was always a little stir in the cantonment. The polo tournament was very popular with the cavalry regiments when other teams came and competed. Guests were put up by the various families. As the bungalows were mostly large enough for the hosts and their own family, a large marquee was put up in each compound, in which, besides beds, the men were given a chest of drawers and a wardrobe. Part of the tent was separated off to be used as a bathroom, such as an officer had when travelling. The nights were still very cold, so each had a fireplace with stove for warmth.

On different occasions throughout the year, each regiment had its own display to which the officers' wives and families were invited and received by the General's wife. I was asked to take Michael who loved watching the horses. In the evenings during the previous weeks, we had strolled on to our small maidan and watched the horses being put through their training. What I have always remembered has been the patience of these soldiers with their horses. When a horse jibbed at a hurdle, the man, without a cross word or action, would repeat, taking the horse backwards and forwards until it had confidence and took the leap.

The weather was now warming up and with our nets well tucked in to keep out the mosquitoes, we were having our beds taken outside and sleeping in the open. Michael's mother was a very good animal painter and had been asked by the "18th" to paint their band horse for the officers' mess. Every morning, an orderly arrived with the horse and all its trappings. These last had been borrowed for studying the necessary details but were to be collected before the weekend. Mike's mother was to be away then and I did not want the responsibility of them, as they were valuable, to be in the house while she and her husband were away. Friday night came and no messenger had arrived so I was asked to hide them somewhere. I felt uneasy about them but hid them at the bottom of a roomy wardrobe with a pile of clothes on top. That was a most amusing weekend. That night I noticed the bed had not been put outside and the nights were too stifling for us to sleep in the house. When I enquired why, my bearer was surprised. I gathered that he did not think it safe for me to be alone outside, however, when I said Whisky and Otto, our dogs, could lie out on my veranda and that our orderly was on the Sahib's veranda, he was reassured and the beds were put out as usual. Whisky was very good but Otto played up and in desperation, I had to take him and his bed into where he always spent the night. I returned and got under my mosquito net and soon got lost in sleep. In the morning, I went along to see if all was well with Otto and was at first rather puzzled because he was nowhere to be seen. I noticed that a sheet on the bed covered a little lump and when I called, "Otto, Otto," amidst a series of groans whines, the sheet going round and round, finally Otto emerged and both sheet and Otto landed on the floor. Poor Otto, he must have been more afraid than I was and wouldn't have been much use if anything had happened!

Arrangements had been made to move up to Kashmir and dates had been fixed when I developed a very sore throat – very common in India and the doctor had been sent for. Being an Indian regiment, the doctor had been drawn from the 1.M.S. He was very conscientious and at first he thought that mine was a case of diptheria. I was sceptical about this as I had had diptheria once if not twice before and felt that I must be immune. However, a swab of my throat was taken. It proved negative but, owing to my condition, our trip was delayed until the doctor gave permission for me to travel. This was given after a week's postponement and we left on 9th May 1935. At 5000 feet, I spent my birthday at an Oak bungalow. My 2nd birthday was spent on a sailing vessel. My birthday in 1922 was in a train from Madras going up the Ghat on our way to Kotagiri. Even on my birthday, I seemed to enjoy travelling, for in 1943, I spent my 59th birthday on board the "Strathaird" from Bombay. I felt very sad as our troopship slipped away for the last time from a country that I had known and loved for so many years – a country full of interest and promise. For me, I knew it meant goodbye and I felt sad. But in 1935, I had not reached the parting of the ways. I was starting out in our car along our wide roads under spreading trees towards Kashmir. We passed Jammu, the winter quarters for the then Maharajah of Kashmir and continued on the marvellously built, zig-zag road up to Srinagar, where after a rest for the night at an Oak bungalow, we were ready to go on with our journey. We spent a few days living on a house-boat on the river until the snow cleared sufficiently to let us continue the rest of the 10,000 feet climb to Gulmarg, on horseback or dandi. The Bannihal pass was built by our Royal engineers and was a monument to their workmanship. It was a single line traffic up and the same going down. At a certain point, every two hours, the ascending traffic would stop to let the descending traffic move. After being closed for winter snow, the road was just beginning to open up and coolies were very busy clearing the snow off the road. It was, I should say, a very dangerous job for as you shovelled the snow off the road, throwing it down the khud, more snow from above would loosen and rush over the road, carrying all before it. We were stopped once or twice by a warning shout from the coolies and while they stood back and we stopped, we fully realised what would have happened had we been foolish enough not to heed their shouts. At one point, a tunnel of hard snow had been formed for us to pass through. I have a photo of the snow piled high which Mike's mother took time to take. After stopping for one night at a Dak bungalow, we reached Srinagar. Picture Venice in Kashmir and you may have a slight idea of what it is like. There is the river with comfortable house-boats. In them there was a dining room and lounge with sleeping accommodation and tied on at the end is the cook's boat with all he requires – one has one's own servants as at home, who have come up from the plains or are local servants, hired with the boat. Little gondolas, with bearded merchants with blue eyes and pink complexion come alongside and try to tempt you to buy their fascinating selection of goods, which varied from furs, precious stones and leather goods.

Your house-boat had a deck over the living quarters and from there you got a view of the Sun with its shops and houses – all so picturesque – but with the next tremor, you would expect them to collapse like a pack of cards. If tired of looking at Mount Suliman, one could hire a boatman. There were many that plied up and down, only too pleased to take you to the beautiful Shalimar Gardens. Looking at them and wandering around, your thoughts took you back to the time of the great Moguls and you could imagine the ladies of the court, walking along the paths and enjoying the beautiful flowers. During the hot weather, Kashmir was where Court was in residence but when the cool weather came, they trekked by camel and bullock wagon to Delhi.

Another spot I remember is the beautiful, dreamlike, "Dhal Lake". After selecting our boat, we climbed in and were skilfully guided by two boatmen through a whirlpool till we came into smooth water. It made me think of the Blue Lagoon, with water as smooth as a mill pond and snow clad Himalayas all round us. One felt that one was living in Disneyland. The clumps of wax-like lotus flowers were so fairy like and so beautiful. As the boat glided along, one wondered why people should want to fight over so beautiful a land.

After three weeks in Srinagar, we heard that Gulmarg was opening up for visitors so we arranged to move also. To get there, one had to ride on pony or dandy. Mike and I went in the latter. The baggage all went by coolie. As we left Srinagar, we passed through a tall row of poplar trees and then went up and up until we reached Gulmarg. It is a large plateau, circled with tall fir trees and in the shelter of these, cluster the various huts that were hired for the season by Europeans, mostly represented by army, government, missionary and merchant families. There were a few boarding houses and one or two hotels. One that I remember was "Nedows" and there was a boarding house kept by a Miss Christie. All ranks of life seemed to know her. She and a Miss Coburn worked a great deal for the welfare of the coolie but she always kept a favourite spot in her heart for Scots people. I believe her father was a farmer in Perthshire and she loved meeting anyone Scottish. On arriving at Gulmarg, I received an introduction to her and all the time I was in India until the war – 11 years – I was indebted to her tor her kindness and hospitality. Our bungalow was one of those owned by her. At that time, a Scottish missionary was staying at "Harramuck" which was her guest house. I remember one or two picnics that were organised for this girl and myself. We were provided with a packed basket full of cold roast chicken, curry puffs, salad, cold drinks and coffee. Each of us rode on a pony that had a syce to lead it. My pony was a beautiful, well-kept dapple-grey, called George. On this particular day, we went up to Killinmarg. It meant a long ride as it was about 2000 feet higher up than Gulmarg. To help the ponies, large steps were cut out on the khud and of course when we reached our picnic ground, they had their saddle and bridle removed and were allowed to feed and have a long rest. The coolies also enjoyed a meal, rest and possibly a pull at a hookah. The wild flowers and scenery were lovely and it is a day still fresh in my memory.

I can't remember meeting any of the nurses at Gulmarg but there must have been many, for I do know that one day every week, a tennis court at the club, which was at the end of the marg, was reserved for them. Mothers were supposed to look after their families that day but there were always a few officers off duty only too glad to have something to do and no doubt the children enjoyed the lack of discipline. In Nedow there was a small cinema as well as a hotel and on the same night, it was opened for the nurses. It was a unique centre for thinking of the welfare of the nurses. It was in Nedow that a bachelor Colonel showed his love for the children by giving them a party every year while he was stationed there – a party which they eagerly looked forward to and much enjoyed.

To reach the Maidan and these points that I have mentioned, my route from our bungalow lead through the bazaar. It, like the Band Srinagar, was most picturesque but so fragile in structure. Under a small veranda would be seated the owner of each section, booth or shop as you liked to call it. On my time off, I enjoyed wandering through and examining the various goods in wood craft, papier-mâché and silk, Kashmir and fur. What I would have liked would have been some of the precious stones but warned the kind merchant that I had no money to buy. "Never mind, Miss Sahib, come in and look." It was raining and I was only too glad to accept his kind offer and spend an hour until the rain passed off, while on jeweller's sheet after sheet, he laid out priceless opals, pearls, emeralds, rubies, pieces made of jade, moonstones, diamonds and lapis lazuli. I bought three sets of buttons – one in cats-eye, one in lapis-lazuli and one in moss agates, which is supposed to be my birthstone. Another day at a fur shop, I bought a warm pair of lynx gloves which I passed on in a parcel for the Salvation Army only the other day. They were warm but not expensive. I also bought a beautiful pair of gloves in baby leopard skin. They were so soft and perfectly marked and I gave them to an invalid friend of mine as I felt that they would keep her hands so warm. For myself, the leather merchant made to order a shoulder bag. The flap over was in a design which carried out the chingrah leaf of Kashmiri. It was done in coloured thread which brought out the wonderful winter colouring of the maple or chinnah leaf. At the wood stall, I bought a card tray – a single chenar leaf in shesham wood. My sisters sent me a sample of the wallpaper in my bedroom and I consulted with the owner of the papier-mâché stall and he agreed to make a bedside lamp and work in those colours. It was very delicate and I was pleased with the result. I bought a work box in opal colouring for my young sister and a small red box for myself. For my eldest sister I bought a lovely silk shoulder wrap. The ends were in Paisley pattern and ignorantly I said to a friend who was with me, "How cleverly they have copied our Paisley pattern." The shopkeeper evidently knowing English interrupted me to say, "Pardon me, Miss Sahib, but it was your people who copied us." So it was. Our merchants, when in India, had seen and admired the pattern, studied it carefully and on returning to this country, were able to teach it to our weavers in Paisley. Hence the name of those heirlooms that have belonged to our forebears and were worn as shawls or used to cover the backs of our lounge settees.

Before leaving the hills, the walnuts were ready and were being sold at 4 annas (6d.) a hundred!

Bearing in mind that in my time in Kotagiri where my family shared a bungalow with two other families, we managed to live happily together and spent a most enjoyable time. I had looked forward to a repetition of the same when we joined forces in Gulmarg. I soon found out that was not to be so. The parents and the little girl were quite harmless but the nurse was most inconsiderate and made no attempt to fit in with me. I agreed to share my bearer as their bearer was to look after the parents – as they lived in a separate bungalow a little lower down from ours – which consisted of two semi-huts and a veranda. I had agreed as I thought we would all be having our meals together at the same time. I soon discovered that this wasn't the case. Worst of all was when it came to going out. There was no bearer to push my pram. Judy being asleep when Mike and I were having tea, she had now commandeered my bearer to bring her bath whilst I was dressed and waiting to go out. I fear that I was thought unreasonable but I stood my ground and other arrangements had to be made for Judy and her nurse. Unfortunately, and why, I don't know, the bearer who came up with us was upset and wanted to return to the plains. I managed to get a very superior and educated nursery bearer. His father was friendly with Miss Christie and she had paid for his education and taken an interest in him. He served me very well in Gulmarg and remained for some time with me in Sialkot. Unfortunately, he had an uncle in the plains who had a bad influence over him, which lead to his opening my dispatch box and helping himself to money. Mike's father and bearer went to his quarters and it was proved that he was the culprit. I was asked if I wanted to hand him over to justice. He was so young and otherwise had done me well, so I said I would like him sent back to his father in Gulmarg and I would write to Miss Christie. From that, Miss Christie afterwards told me, he gave his father a lot of trouble and continued to be under his uncle's thumb. I was sorry when I heard this because I felt that I should never have taken him down to the plains where life and people were so different to those that he belonged to and was accustomed to in Kashmir.

It was now the end of the hot season and many of the British people were returning to the plains. The family with whom we had shared the bungalow had already gone down to the plains and now Mike's father's leave was up so it was arranged that our bungalow would be given up but for the last ten days. Mike and I were to go to another bungalow and keep another nurse and two little girls company as their parents would also be returning to Sialkot. It was decided that we would all share a truck and, with our luggage, go down the khud together. The bazaar had been closed and Gulmarg had taken on a dismal and deserted look. It was becoming very cold. In fact, on the day we left, there was a sprinkling of snow and going down the khud, we experienced such a cutting wind that my chin began to bleed. We became enveloped in such a terrifying mist that we were unable to see the driver or his mate. We just heard the latter assuring the driver that we were still on the road. As we crawled along, we came to a stand post and at this one, were two or three policemen. The senior one told us that we could go no further and that we must stop there for the night. The Oak bungalow where we had booked accommodation was lower down the khud, so we were directed to another bungalow but, as we expected, we were told it was full up. As we were all shivering with the cold, I said to the caretaker that he must let us shelter somewhere as we had two small children and I had a baby. Sympathetically, he said that he would go and talk to the others in the Oak. It is when you are abroad that you realise the kindness of your people. I don't know who we were sharing with that night but they were quite of one mind that they would dine on the veranda and we were to have the dining room. We had to share three charpoys which we made as comfortable to sleep on as we could. Two of the children shared one and Mike lay at the end of mine. This room of course had no bathroom, as one had when renting a room under normal conditions, but a lady showed her thoughtfulness by saying that we were to make use of hers whenever we liked, for the children and ourselves. The khansama was able to give us some suitable meal at night and after an early breakfast, we were able to continue our journey down the road with many hairpin bends until we reached the plains, where, under the shade of a spreading peepal tree, we opened our ice-box and had a picnic lunch. By now it was like a very warm day at home. We dropped the other family towards evening and were happy to get back to our bungalow, where we were given a warm welcome.

During this time in India, Quetta had a terrible earthquake when much was demolished. Our old bungalow, I believe, and part of the Scottish Church and much of the bazaar was brought to rubble. The Chinaman, who made my shoes, and his wife lost all their seven children. Afterwards I found they had moved up to Simla and now had another baby girl who was christened in the English Church. His wife was a Christian and we always stopped to talk to baby Barbara, who would be lying in her pram outside the shop door. I don't fancy that religion troubled John Chinaman. When not making his beautiful shoes, we said that he spent his playing mah-jong with his companions. Thirty four years ago! I wonder what happened to little Barbara and her pretty little mother. So much has happened in India since she left the protection of Britain and our Empire began to crumble. Did our brave King see some cracks in the wall? It was a sad day to us all, for in the whole British Empire, their loyal citizens showed their grief. A service was held in the little Regimental Church on the maidan at Sialkot. Interesting for me, for it was in that church that one of my old boys was christened in 1902. His father at that time was M. O. for the Brigade. Mike's father said that I should be there and for Mike to sit in his pram outside the church. The church was packed and I was struck by the number of Indian officers who entered the building and sat down with British officers. Some of them may have, or if too young, their fathers may have been in France with the Indian troops and seen our King when he visited the trenches during War 1. I remember a gun was fired, the last post was sounded and then with muffled drums, the soldiers marched away. It was an impressive service and one to be remembered. I walked round the inside of this church and stopped to read below a memorial, alas, of a young officer who had been killed at polo, the words, "In the midst of life is death." Often we had heard of the supernatural polo player that haunted the maidan.

For most of us during these days, life went on in the same way. My Missionary friends invited me to spend Christmas Eve with them and I was able to see how the Christian children entered into singing our Christmas carols in Punjabi, then each received a present. It was sweet to watch the young ones hugging a doll just as one of our children would. I would have remained for Christmas Day but as Mike's parents were having friends for dinner, I had to refuse that. I was very lucky knowing these Scottish women, for through knowing them, I made other friends. Two or three I still keep up with and am interested in hearing of others that I had known. As one gets old, it is difficult to keep up as one once did. One gives way to laziness – is it? Or is it that one lacks energy? I hope that I have that excuse.

While with Mike, I remember the bearer coming to inform me that there was a snake charmer in the compound and would I like to go out and watch him. Mike was sound asleep in his pram and well-guarded by a servant, so I agreed to the see old man coming onto the veranda and letting me see how he could charm. Snakes are believed to go about in pairs, so when he produced one, I asked to see the mate and after playing on his pipe, the mate appeared. I can't remember the names of them all but I remember there was a kreit, a russell viper, a python and then he came to a cobra. He shook his head and said he was sorry but he was unable to produce the mate. I think I had promised a rupee, so I said that if the mate appeared, I would give him an extra rupee. After much blowing on the pipe, through a hole separating the wall between the compound where I was sitting, and the small maidan, I saw an evil looking head appear. No wonder that Satan is likened to a serpent. It was an evil sight. It was securely placed in the round basket with the other species. I parted with my two rupees, the old man salaamed and moved on, leaving that day as one other to remember.

Michael had wakened up and after a wash and a clean suit, we were ready for tea on the lawn and then a walk on the maidan before returning for bedtime, after which, I would enjoy my bath before my dinner arrived and I settled down for the evening. Occasionally I would have the Mission ladies over from Barrah Pattar for tea on the lawn. Mike was with his parents and I was able to go for a car run as far as Jammu, where the Hindu ruler of Kashmir had his cold weather palace. Now that part is Indian and Sialkot is Pakistan. The Maharajahs have abdicated and the "Winds have changed." The barrier that now exists would no longer allow of that lovely run along a wide road, shaded by spreading leafy trees. How glad I am that I knew India as it was.

This last cold weather, we had a young lady staying with us. I fancy that she had come out from home for the season and was under the care of Mike's mother. It was arranged that she was to travel with us. Mike's father was following shortly afterwards. We were travelling across France from Marseilles to Calais and I remember they had bought a good supply of cigarettes at Simon Artz's shop in Port Said and were wondering what to do with them when going through the customs. They laughed, for knowing me to be a non-smoker, presented me with an opened packed. Mike's mother was a heavy smoker so soon got through the other and then fell back on mine! We spent one night at Paris. The part of Paris that one sees when travelling is not very attractive. The streets are so narrow and, of course, one does not have enough time for more than a glimpse.

Dover was not far from where Michael's maternal grandparents lived and where we were to make our headquarters. As I was not staying in this post now that I had returned to Britain with Michael, I was looking out for another job that would take me back to India. Mike's father motored us to Brighton where his mother was living at that time. She was anxious to have the little boy to stay with her and thought it wise to have him with her before I left, as she realised children take a little time to get accustomed to new nurses with their new ways. I knew Brighton very well and both Mike and I liked staying with his grandmother. While I was there, I applied to an advertisement which I thought I would like. It was for a first baby and was for Simla. I had seen Madras with its tropical beauty, I had seen Quetta guarding the north and I had seen Amballa and Sialkot, full of Munity history. I had seen Sukkur, one of the two hottest places in India where the first Goffer Dam was built to help to irrigate the salt parched land of Sind. I had seen, during their hot weather, Karachi – a delightful port and town by the sea, with Risalpur on the wild frontier where there were two mounted regiments and a good air force which made us feel well protected from border raids. There is something about the frontier that calls you. It may have been in answer to that call that I applied for the post and in answer, the grandmother-to-be and her daughter came to see me. Mike was with me during the interview and I remember how drawn the ladies were to him. Certainly he was a dear and well-behaved little fellow. We discussed what the post would be like and as the infant was not expected for a short time, it would give me time to take a holiday in Scotland with my sisters and see to my wardrobe for another period in India. This time it was to be for three years. "Man proposes and God disposes." Because of World War II, it was seven years before I saw my people and homeland.

When I was in Sukkur, I had become friends with the only other nurse living there – a friendship which we kept up for many years. She took over a family of mine who were living at Folkestone, which is not far from Dover and, whilst still with Mike, she came over to have tea with me and to get news of my new move. She was very interested to hear about it because she had been with an uncle of the infant-to-be and had charge of Barbara when she was a baby.

I was in Scotland when I heard of the arrival of the baby and, early in June, I arrived at Welbeck Street home to take over this first and precious grandchild. Her grandmother was there and drove mother, infant and nurse to stay with her at Petworth, which was home for the next two months, when the father was to arrive on leave from India. This house had a lovely walled garden where I used to spend much of my spare time. While we were with the grandparents, the baby was christened in the lovely old church at Petworth which was in the village and close to our garden wall. From my nursery window, I looked over the wall to Petworth House estate. I did not see the house which harboured a priceless and famous collection of pictures. I believe now, the public have permission to view them. In August, we stayed in a small house that had been rented in Rustington, near the house where I had stayed when with Christopher, Sheila and her young sister. At this time, Miss Maylott was having a holiday and was pleased to spend a week with me. I was able to get a room for her and we met during the day. Time was passing quickly. We would have to find another place to go to for the house had only been let for a certain time and our time for leaving was drawing near. Hove was thought of but, on making enquiries, no-one seemed to want a baby and certainly not if accompanied by a nurse! However we managed to find comfortable rooms at a small hotel in one of the streets leading down to the beach. We spent Christmas there and in January we went to live at a relative's house that was closing as the owner, an old cousin, had died. It was nice being in

London before sailing for I was able to say goodbye to my cousins. Two very dear friends who I had been with, in charge of their son who was now posted for India, would be going there with his wife shortly. While in India, this time I met them in Amballa and later during War II, in Nathia Ghali. At that time, they had a little daughter of two years.

I was also able to re-unite with a friend of my childhood whom I had not seen for some years. She was a widow and lived in Wimbledon and worked at the Asiastic Library. She was very clever and had been able to lead a very interesting career. It was a very happy reunion and in a few meetings, we were able to have many interesting talks.

Before leaving Rustington, I had an invitation to visit Mike's grandmother who was staying in a boarding house in Bournemouth. Miss Mayloft was alone at this time in Folkestone so it was arranged that I was to spend a few days with her and take a bus from Rye which would take me to Bournemouth. It was a very enjoyable few days with two people who were to pass out of my life – like ships in the night. I had strange misgivings about going to Simla. Mike's grandmother advised me not to think of it and, later while in India, I heard from her, enquiring if I had settled down or if I would consider being her companion and help her with the running of a small house. If I had thought of it, I was not in a position to consider it.

Just before leaving London, we listened into the wireless and heard Edward VIII giving his sad parting speech to the nation. Knowing how he was loved by us all and how in the past he had cast a charm on all his subjects, in all stations of life, it came as a great shock and caused grief to the nation.

We left Tilbury on the old Kaiser Hind. It had been a prize in War I and was torpedoed in War II. In 1937, it had reached a rather dirty and dilapidated stage. However when we reached Marseilles, we were transferred to the "Strathaird" which was quite new. My family had relations seeing them off.

We had a smooth trip with two days at Marseilles and again stopping at Port Said. As we steamed towards the latter port, The "Vanguard" was recognised by the stewards and everyone went to the side of the "Strathaird" to have a closer look at this giant air-carrier. I did not think that in two more years we would be at war and she would be in action, nor, as I walked round Simon Artz, that it was for the last time and that I would never see again the lovely bougainvillea which I admired so much and always associated with Port Said. About a hundred American Missionaries embarked at Port Said on their way to India. They surrounded my baby's pram and worshipped her calling her "the smiling baby" and imploring me always to be kind to her! This injunction rather entertained me. As always, I enjoyed slipping down the Canal and admiring the lovely sky effects at night, there again not realising that this journey was not to be repeated in my future. I never gave way to crystal-gazing and doubt if I would have found it helpful to know my future.

We arrived in Bombay and waited for various officials to come on board. When they were satisfied and we had shown our passports, we disembarked. I think that we were putting up at the Metropole until we left by the G.P.R. I shared my apartment with a very nice young lady who was going to meet her husband. My baby Margaret was very good and gave no trouble. Until Lahore, the journey was familiar. After that it was among the Simla hills and finally a long, zig-zag motor run to just below Simla, where we had to travel by tonga. The Viceroy was the only person allowed to travel by motor in Simla itself. Simla was the summer quarters for the Viceroy and his suite, and the Governor of Bombay and his retinue. "Sherfield" was the name of the bungalow where we were to live. In the top lived a Mr. Potiphar with his son and their servants. This Indian gentleman was as if he had come out of a Kipling novel and was seldom seen or heard and very harmless. Our part of the bungalow had a large veranda from where one had a marvellous view. From my window away from the veranda, one looked towards vice-regal lodge. Further up the khud, one came to lovely houses occupied by seniors in the Civil Service and at the end was where the Governor of Bombay lived. As you went along, you passed the Senior Medical Officer's bungalow. (I found he was a cousin of mine and I enjoyed the friendship and hospitality that he and his wife showed to me.) Near to them was the hospital and lower down was the secretariat. From each of these ran a winding perpendicular street with links with each building. On this street was the "Green Room" which was a kind of club used by the residents for meeting in. They used it when they were holding theatricals etc. There was also a Swiss cafe that was very popular. There were two Chinese shops that were also popular. At one, I bought my Chinese amber necklace and one called a beggar's necklace. I also got some Chinese china animals. Unfortunately through time, they all, except for one green horse, got broken. The other shop was owned by the Chinaman, father of Barbara, who lost all his seven children at one time in the Quetta earthquake as I've already mentioned. He continued to make my shoes until

I left India. I have often missed him for the shoes were always so comfortable.

Not far from there was the English Church. The Church of Scotland closed during the cold weather so I always attended the English Church. The vicar had an English nurse to look after their children. Although many families had moved down to Delhi, there were many families still staying with their children in the hills. You felt belonging to a smaller and friendlier circle. My family hired a car driver to meet us and take us on a lovely tour. First, we put up at a hotel in Delhi, the new Capital designed by Lutyens and Herbert Baker – a Capital worthy of our Great Empire. One wonders if it now draws the admiration and appreciation it deserves. Margaret's mother very kindly said that she would take charge of the little girl and that I was to have the use of the car and driver for one of the days that we were to be in New Delhi. I was more than delighted and got in touch with a nurse who I was very friendly with. She was one of those who moved to Delhi in the winter and who knew the ropes. After running round and getting a bird's eye view of the new Capital, we entered the old city. "Lest we forget," was where Britain's sons and heroes lie buried on the hillside looking over the city where they fought and died at the time of the Mutiny. There was the little church built to the memory of Skinner's horse. On its walls are tablets to men and officers of Uiat regiment who died and were killed during that time. There, in the centre of the city, rises a tall memorial to Nicholson, the hero of Delhi. It was said that his men wept when they knew that their officer whom they loved, had been killed. I enjoyed going through the brass bazaar and looking at all the beautiful bowls and vases that were made by the Indians.

The fort dated back to Akbar, the first great Mogul king who came across the mountains from Persia and conquered India. The fort was a very imposing and interesting building. I also saw a beautiful mosque but time was wearing on and, after tea with my friend, I returned to the hotel to take care of my charge. Next morning, we left New Delhi and continued our tour. Going on our way to Agra, we passed the palace of Fatehpur Sikri. To my mind it was much more beautiful than the Taj Mahal. After building it, the architect realised that there was no adequate water supply so had to move to another site where water could be obtained, which was why the Taj Mahal was built. It was magnificent. The walls are of alabaster, inlaid with mosaic and precious stones. They were selling some chips and I was able to buy a little ash tray and buttons made from lapis lazuli. My employers wanted to continue to central India, so the little girl was left with me at the hotel until their return.

Every afternoon we had our tea under a tree in the compound. The dear little squirrels used to come and enjoy the crumbs that we threw to them. One with brown tinges, we called Ginger. They were most daring, sitting on my lap or the tyre of the pram wheel, eating cake crumbs. One day, I was startled by a mongoose rushing out of our bathroom. The servants found no serpent, so the mongoose must have dispatched him or driven him out of the bathroom, so I felt reassured. In a few days, the parents returned and we retraced our steps to Simla. At the end of another hot season, when the theatricals and tournaments came to an end, the staffs were moved to New Delhi and the cantonment became very quiet with a brown bear feeling of going to sleep for the winter.

Margaret's mother decided to go home to her own people for a while and I was given the chance of going home or remaining. If I had decided on going home, Margaret would have had an ayah. An ayah and no Memsahib seemed unkind to the baby, who I knew would miss us both, so I decided to stay.

When Margaret was two and a half years of age, she got her first pony. It was called Sherry. Margaret's hair was sherry coloured and this pony's name was a perfect match for it, but as he was naughty and shied, we did not keep him. Various ponies came round for our inspection and, one day, a pony with a sweet little face and enveloped in a huge horse blanket appeared. Margaret and I both fell to her but on moving the blanket, Margaret's father said it was just a skeleton. Margaret and I were very disappointed so he relented and said we would take it. Our syce was sure that with good feeding and treatment she would become a good little pony. At one time she must have been a good English pony but had fallen into cruel and unkind hands. I asked the boy what her name was. "Kuch Ney," was the reply. We called her Shelagh. Margaret's only complaint was that she was not as big as Daddy's horse! The pony and the little girl were great pals and loved each other. She was a strawberry roan and with good care and feeding, became a pretty, much admired pony. She was very gentle and Margaret was able to ride her by herself. One day I heard a great peal of laughter. Our nursery lead off the veranda and when I went to investigate, I discovered both pony and child in the nursery!

At the bottom of Simla was a large, flat piece of ground called Annandale. The races and gymkhana were held there. During the season, the children's ponies were inspected and Margaret entered on Shelagh. As her father wished me to walk beside the pony, she was unable to be judged in the competition, although the judges let her walk with the others round the field. It was an experience for her! Next year, she was invited with the other children to attend the party at Vice Regal Lodge. In a white silk frock and her chestnut hair in ringlets, she looked very pretty and was so sweet as she tried to curtsey. It was war time and the parents had all of their children from home for safety. Some of them were big boys who wolfed off cakes and goodies before the small fry had any chance! The nurses and ayahs had to collect what would be nice for their charges so that everyone had fair play. There was a cinema show but I think the little ones would rather have had games and switch backs to play on as they had had at the Club party. On leaving, the children had an ice cream. Unfortunately, Margaret did not like ice cream. We drove home in a rickshaw. An aide-de-camp said goodbye and saw everyone away.

The weather in the plains becoming, the Viceroy and his staff went down to Delhi. Those officers who could, closed their houses in the hills and followed with their families. The Governor of Bengal and his staff also left. Margaret loved visiting the residences now shut up because they had lovely grounds for resting Shelagh, whilst we had tea before returning home. I remember one of the houses was called "Four Winds".

We had a lovely view of the small hills all round. Kasauli and Simla could be seen in the distance. When Lord Kitchener was Commander-in-Chief in India, although "Snowdon" was his official residence, he preferred to live at "Wild Flower Hall". As you can imagine, a place with such a name must be very lovely. I thought so when I first saw it and every birthday, Margaret and I went there on 10th May or the 16th. After Kitchener's time, a Miss Hotz bought it and ran it as a hotel. Just beyond the hotel was a little bungalow that drew my attention. On the gate was a nameplate bearing the name, "Bendochy". The bungalow faced over to hills that might well have been Bridge of Cally. Some time after, we were spending the day with a family friend at the hotel and she told me that Miss Hotz lived there and used it as her retreat when she was tired of the hotel duties. On being introduced to Miss Hotz, I told her that the name on the gate drew my attention, as my married sister lived near Bendochy, a small village in Scotland. She told me that when she bought the bungalow, the agent told her that a young man had had it built for his future bride whom he had hoped to bring to live in it. Unfortunately, two days before they were to sail for India, she was suddenly taken ill and later she died. Naturally, he never wanted to live in it, so it went on the market and Miss Hotz bought it. I have often thought about and wondered who the young man was.

The next year I had a holiday at Narkandah where I spent a delightful time with a few friends at a Church rest house. We had our breakfast in sunshine on a veranda facing the Himalayas which were covered in snow. It was a panorama to be remembered. Going from Simla, it was a distance of about forty miles. I joined the party two days later and with four coolies, we went by rickshaw, breaking the journey for one night at a Dak bungalow. We went past such lovely forests of deodar trees. It was apple time and the orchards were laden with lovely rosy apples which were a change and a great treat from what we could get in Simla. On our way home with five rickshaws, we broke the journey again. We were a jolly party. One of us had a camera and took us in our ricks stationed all in a row. We also passed the little bungalow and I asked the girl if she would take a photograph of "Bendochy". I have the photograph among my collection. This was 1939.

Fortunately Margaret's mother was just in time to get back with her father to India before War II had been declared. The ladies and gentlemen were very busy holding theatricals. Gilbert and Sulivan's "Pirates of Penzance" was being acted and I remember Margaret's mother looked so pretty in a lavender sunbonnet. Friends of mine said how like Margaret was to her mother.

Great changes were taking place in Simla. Some families went to England and others arrived. We were ordered to Abbottabad. Having been with the families of Gurkha officers, I had often heard of it. It is up on the frontier of India midst wild and hilly country.

Margaret and I with Ghazi, our bearer, left in advance. Khitmighar was to follow with Sahib and Mem Sahib. Faithful peno, our nursery bearer had to be parted with. He was a hillman and would not have been happy away from his own people. Sahib's bearer travelled with us as we went first by rickshaw and then by car to catch the train at Tazilla – a historical town, dating back to the days of Alexander the Great. Our train took us as far as Rawalpindi where we engaged a motor to take us to Abbottabad which was seventy miles from Pindi. It was dark by now and it was rather startling to have the light of a hurricane lamp shone in our faces while an officer with a revolver questioned the bearer and searched our car. However, we satisfied the two officers and were allowed to continue on our way to what was to be our home for the next three years.

Abbottabad was the home of the 5th and 6th Gurkhas. Our bungalow, which we afterwards were to live in, backed on to their mess and every night at 8 p.m. a Gurkha would play on his pipes during the officers' dinner hour. It was not so much the bungalow that I enjoyed, it was like any other in the cantonment, but the compound had such space with lovely fruit trees. Soon after we arrived in Abbottabad, a little baby sister arrived and I often think of our little summer house under a cherry tree where, on a charpoy, she would roll and crawl.

A pony was not easy to find but after a short time, we heard of a good pony that belonged to the vet's little boy. He was called "Winkle" and Margaret grew very fond of him – as did her baby sister as she grew older. War was still on so that in odd moments, I would slip into the Club and join the Red Cross ladies to wind bandages and make swabs.

At this time, a small school was started by a lady in Abbottabad. Before her marriage, she had been a trained teacher and Margaret and most of the children of kindergarten age, went to it. It was very nice for Margaret because she was able to make several friends. As she was at school for three hours, it gave me the opportunity of offering my services to the Army Hospital for those hours. I had passed my exams in nursing and first aid, so that when the Colonel asked for recruits from our Ambulance Brigade, we were pleased to be accepted. At first there were only four of us, shepherded by our Superintendent. Two of us worked in the British branch and two of us in the Indian. Later, two more joined so there was one to help in the theatre with our Superintendent and one as a dietician. Even though we had two orderlies in the Indian branch in which I worked, we found it hard work to give each patient all the service he required. "Brass hats" came round to inspect the hospital and we did feel rewarded when our Colonel told us that they had said that our hospital was the only one in India that was run by the St. John's Ambulance Corps. We were glad, when in May 1942, a matron and Queen Alexandra's reserve arrived from England. Naturally they became our seniors but, almost immediately, our Superintendent had trained us and given us plenty of scope to show our skill. Abbottabad was a depot for the 10th Army. Some of our patients were Gurkhas and one could not but admire how brave they were over their wounds. Their officers assured us that they could not say enough of their thanks and appreciation for what we were doing.

Time was broken and passed in many ways. I was able to have a few days in a beautiful place called Nathia Gali with a clergyman and his wife who were at Abbottabad when we first arrived. There were parties at our Army headquarters and the Club for the children.

Early in 1942, word came that we had to leave our lovely bungalow and go to a bungalow in camp as we were marked down for going home. In April, 1943 we left the camp and put up at a small hotel, waiting until we heard of berths in a ship for home. While at the hotel, I heard that three nurses would be leaving for the front. I waited at the gate for the ambulance and was just able to wish them all the best. Everywhere, it was all a case of "Hush, hush". There was little that could pass between us. I am glad to say that all three came safely back, although, to my knowledge, one was one of the few women who was under fire and afterwards won the Burma Medal.

Two days after, we also slipped away as a "Ship in the Night," again finding our way down in an Army truck to Taxilla and hence to Bombay by train. The train journey was terribly hot and it was very difficult to keep the children cool. Indians had become unfriendly. The train was crowded by officers and I found it very difficult to get ice. They paid no attention to our bearer and he, wise man, complained to Sahib who gave us all the ice that went with his whisky pegs. I have often felt that many of the officers would have offered me their share if they had realised how my little girls were suffering from the heat. We were unable to find rooms in any hotel so we spent the night on the "Devonshire" that was lying in the harbour. It was an awful experience. With no fans going and all portholes blacked out, the heat was worse than ever. We lay on the cabin floor as this was the coolest spot. I bathed the youngest child with iced water and when it became warm, rang the steward to bring more. She cried the whole night. I think someone must have reported being unable to sleep because, at last, the steward came round to say that the order had gone round that all portholes were to be opened, as in harbour there was no need for a blackout. Next morning, the doctor enquired how we had fared and said that if he had known, he would have allowed us up on deck. It took the little girl some time to get over the effects and my cabin steward advised me to get a chit from the doctor for ice. As it was difficult with so many men on board to get ice, I was only too thankful to take his advice. It was then decided that we were to travel on the "Strathaird" which was to take us as far as Durban, so all our luggage had to be transferred. Our time at

Durban was very enjoyable. It was a pleasant time of the year and the children enjoyed playing on the beach. The soldiers went to camp and the families were split up among the various hotels. We had no idea when we would get on a ship to return to Britain. One lady on the beach told me that she had waited two years. The food that we were having was a nice change. Vegetable salad and fruit salads were unforgettable.

Each day we would watch the ships as they sailed towards the harbour and hope that it would be the one that we were waiting for. We saw France's largest boat come and go.

I thought of the day in the Sisters' room at Abbottabad when Sister Goodall read our tea cups. There was no word then of leaving Abbottabad. The interpretation of my tea cup was that I would go on a sea voyage with a ship that had one funnel. Was this the ship? It was morning and when by 3 o'clock no word had come, my hopes fell, and especially when I met some fellow passengers from another hotel who whispered to me that they had had word and were going on it. The children's bed hour came and as still no word had come. I unpacked my suitcases which always stood packed ready for departure and went for a bath. On my return, Margaret said that her father wanted to see me. This was to say that we had to see the doctor next morning at 10 a.m. and be on board at 1 p.m. The ship I had seen with one funnel was sailing at 3 p.m. We had breakfast as usual and overheard a whispered conversation between a steward and a man at table. I caught "……sails at 3 p.m." I thought of these words afterwards because we had scarcely all got on board when gangways were raised and one realised that the engines had been running and we were slowly moving out of the harbour at 1 p.m. – two hours before scheduled time. We never found why; one had just to wonder but Durban harboured many shady characters at that time and possibly many not have been friendly to Britain. We lost some of our bedding and other passengers lost possessions also, in spite of being well warned by the General on our ship when leaving Bombay. The "Orion" was a magnificent boat but, being used as a troop ship, we were simply packed. Every night, looking out of our porthole, we saw that men (Polish airmen) were lying almost shoulder to shoulder. I fancy that catering for so many was difficult and water could only be obtained at certain times for morning and evening baths. It taught one to be quick for, in a half hour, I had to bath the two children and myself.

As we passed Cape of Good Hope, we kept near to shore and were escorted by aircraft. As we were so close, we had a splendid view of Table Mountain. We stopped at Freetown, but before we entered the harbour, we gave a shudder as we saw the wreck of a submarine. That night, as I sat down to dinner beside my commander and table companion, he gently said, "Madam, you have forgotten to wear your lifebelt." At night, we slept with them by our bedside and by day, I had to guard two for the children and my own, wherever we were. An officer said that we might go down in three minutes so we realised how careful we had to be. Fortunately, we had a British crew so that even with such a crowded boat, we felt that there would be no panic on board – that, as in the past, it would still be women and children first. My quick reply brought a laugh round the table. "I fear, sir, that you can't have noticed that we have crossed the bar?" As we crossed the bar, we knew we were safe from torpedoes and we were told, while inside harbour, lifebelts were not necessary. It was such a relief and rest not to lag them round. The passengers were not allowed ashore at Freetown but some of the ship's officers went to the bazaar and brought back those woven baskets that are made by the natives and we find so useful for carrying our purchases in when going for our daily shopping.

The trees and foliage that we saw from our steamer were very green and tropical looking and reminded me of what one saw round Madras. After two days we left Freetown and the temperature seemed more bearable. One day, we seemed to alter our course and everyone wondered why and where we were going. One or two wondered if we were making for Canada. Then land appeared, which to some of the passengers was familiar. After passing what turned out to be the north of Ireland, we drew near the west coast of Scotland. Many wondered if we would enter the Clyde but, on we sailed, past Paddy's Milestone we went, then the sailors became busy. The swimming pool was emptied and a great barrage balloon was erected. There was thick fog so we could see nothing and all the time we heard the constant booming of the fog horn as we slowly and carefully sailed up the river to where we knew must be Liverpool. On the purser's board was announced that no-one was to go ashore until passed by the doctor. The names of various hotels were mentioned but against each name was written, "All Full". In India it was such a common thing to pass a night in a waiting room that I did not worry. We would do just that and catch the first train for Scotland. When I showed our passports, the inspector, on hearing of my plans, said, "I think that I can do something better than that for you if you wait while I speak to this gentleman." Pointing to a man near us. After a few words, the gentleman said that the last train for Scotland had left but he was arranging for us to be put up for the night. A W.R.A.C. drove up in a car and after receiving an order, we whizzed along street after street. The name plates had all been removed so, to this day, I do not know in what street I spent the night, but I shall never forget the kindness shown to us and some of our fellow passengers. We drew up at a tall city house and when the door was opened, it was like entering fairy land. In the first room were some that I recognised as those whom we had lived with on board the "Orion" these last few weeks. In the next room were some of the children that we had seen on the boat – some on a rocking horse, bigger ones looking at books or engaged in playing snakes and ladders or similar games. The girls and I had a cup of Bovril, then we were told to come and see where we were to sleep. A lady and two children that we knew on board suggested it would be nice for us all to share the room, which I was glad to agree to. We afterwards went down to a large room where a generous cold supper was laid out. I had warned my sister in my last letters that I would be making for Scotland and hoped she would be able to put us up until we were able to make permanent plans for our home. Now that I was in England, the difficulty was to get in touch with my sister. The lady who was my hostess said that I must get in touch with the police. That sounded dreadful but that was how it was done in 1943. The police rang up the police in Perthshire and contacted my sister, putting me through so that we were able to speak to one another. Everything was hush hush. A lady came to me and said that her husband had been taken to hospital and she had no idea which hospital he was in, nor could she give him any idea where she was staying. I was able to tell her how the police had helped me to contact my sister and later she told me that they had also helped her and she had been taken to see her husband in hospital.

We had received news of the departure of our train for the North. It meant an early breakfast and the kind gentleman who had befriended us on our landing at Liverpool was ready, waiting to escort and see us off at the railway station. I told them how kind they were being to us. He only shrugged his shoulders and said, "It is all in the day's work. Whenever a boat arrives, some of our people are there to meet it and see what we can do to help." This was one of the many instances of kindness and help that was shown by the police and W.V.S. in Liverpool during War II. We were also grateful for the large packet of sandwiches that we were provided with.

After a tiring journey, we reached Edinburgh where we were to break the journey for a few days. After being overseas for seven years, it was lovely to be home and stay with my two sisters. It was harvest time and my little girls were very interested watching the harvest being taken in. It was a very happy time until Margaret went to school. It was our first break and we both felt it. She was seven years old. Later, I went to stay at Warsash to live with an uncle – taking Bridget with me. The girls' father had a job there for a few months and afterwards worked for the Navy on one of the small ships. Bridget was parked at the school Margaret was at until I was able to get a house. I went and lived with my married sister and together the two of us went house hunting. We managed to find one within reasonable distance of Margaret's school, so Bridget was able to come to our new home and Margaret came during the holidays. Their father was overseas for the first few years. The house was a long, rambling building but it just suited me because, in the summer months, I was able to have a few summer visitors. The front door opened on to the village street but from a sunny porch at the back, you looked on to a lovely stretch of garden which sloped gently down to an orchard along the foot of which ran a small burn. Under the windows facing south, we grew flowers and roses. We had a good lawn which was separated from the hens and vegetables. A thick hedge sheltered us from the East wind. We enjoyed sitting and having tea in a little summer house which was shaded from the sun by a tall oak tree. Along by the hedge was an ash tree and at the burn, a beautiful chestnut which was the first to open its leaves. On the other side of the burn was a field belonging to a farmer and beyond that, we had an uninterrupted view of the Sidlaw hills. In a corner of the garden where the gooseberries grew was a weeping elm, where on its branches a pair of wood pigeons used to coo at dawn. Beside our hen house – it was a converted wash house – was a three stall stable and adjoining coach house. I believe a previous owner drove a pair of horses and kept a hack for riding. When we bought "Graybank", coal and logs were occupying the stalls and the coach house, although the saddle rack was still there, was being used to harbour the family car. We, not owning a car, found it useful for storing boxes and junk.

We must have spent ten years in "Graybank" and looking back, I feel that we all thought them happy years. I feel that this is where I would like to bring my dialogue to a close.